SAFE BY DESIGN:

Designing Safety in Health Care Facilities, Processes, and Culture

BY JOHN REILING, M.H.A., M.B.A., PH.D.

Improving Health Care Quality and Safety

Editor: Cecily Pew
Senior Project Manager: Cheryl Firestone
Associate Director, Production: Johanna Harris
Associate Director, Editorial Development: Cecily Pew
Executive Director: Catherine Chopp Hinckley
Vice President, Learning: Charles Macfarlane, F.A.C.H.E.
Joint Commission/JCR Reviewers: Rick Croteau, John Fishbeck, Jerry Gervais

Joint Commission Resources Mission
The mission of Joint Commission Resources is to continuously improve the safety and quality of care in the United States and in the international community through the provision of education and consultation services and international accreditation.

Joint Commission Resources educational programs and publications support, but are separate from, the accreditation activities of The Joint Commission. Attendees at Joint Commission Resources educational programs and purchasers of Joint Commission Resources publications receive no special consideration or treatment in, or confidential information about, the accreditation process.

The inclusion of an organization name, product, or service in a Joint Commission publication should not be construed as an endorsement of such organization, product, or service, nor is failure to include an organization name, product, or service to be construed as disapproval.

This publication is designed to provide accurate and authoritative information in regard to the subject matter covered. Every attempt has been made to ensure accuracy at the time of publication; however, please note that laws, regulations, and standards are subject to change. Please also note that some of the examples in this publication are specific to the laws and regulations of the locality of the facility. The information and examples in this publication are provided with the understanding that the publisher is not engaged in providing medical, legal, or other professional advice. If any such assistance is desired, the services of a competent professional person should be sought.

Printed in the U.S.A. 5 4 3 2 1

Requests for permission to make copies of any part of this work should be mailed to
Permissions Editor
Department of Publications
Joint Commission Resources
One Renaissance Boulevard
Oakbrook Terrace, Illinois 60181
permissions@jcrinc.com

ISBN: 978-1-59940-104-1
Library of Congress Control Number: 2007930609

For more information about Joint Commission Resources, please visit http://www.jcrinc.com.

Cover photo credit: Single Patient Room, St. Joseph's Hospital, West Bend, Wisconsin. Used with permission.

Contents

Foreword

Internalizing safety as a serious and crucial issue in hospital design was not an immediately obvious or simple process for a health care administrator such as myself, even with my 30 years' experience in the operation of hospitals and health care organizations. But evidence of the amount of patient harm occurring in health care organizations was mounting, and the issue of patient safety in facility design began attracting interest. In 1999 the Institute of Medicine published *To Err Is Human: Building a Safer Health System*, a document that did much to raise awareness about the preventable harm that was happening to patients in hospitals, despite the rapid increase in life-saving and life-extending technologies and procedures.

In 2002 I was president/CEO of St. Joseph's Hospital in West Bend, Wisconsin and we were about to embark on a replacement hospital project when we became intrigued by the question: Could the design of a hospital, with its technology and equipment, be planned to optimize patient safety? Although I had already been involved with hundreds of millions of dollars of hospital construction, including four replacement hospitals, this question had never been asked, as far as I was aware.

While researching the topic, it became apparent that there was little or no literature on the topic of hospital facility development focused specifically on patient safety. An informal survey of health organizations and associations throughout the country that were active in patient safety could not provide advice that directly answered the question, although many had personal anecdotes about how the design of a hospital facility affected their performance within it. One physician discussed how a noisy emergency department could lead to an inability to concentrate, causing slips, lapses, and mistakes. Another physician mentioned that the poor design of medication storage in an intensive care unit can make it easy to grab the wrong dosage of a certain drug. All the persons contacted during our research supported the concept of facilities designed for safety, yet none could give direction on how this could be accomplished.

Out of these collectively recognized concerns, and from the realization that safety by design was a substantive subject, the National Learning Lab was born April 2002, in Milwaukee, Wisconsin. Its goal was to create definitions and a road map for safety by design, including safe design principles, process recommendations, and an enhanced safety culture using facility design.

In so doing, the National Learning Lab created an opportunity for an organization to follow its recommendations. St. Joseph's Hospital, the key sponsor of the National Learning Lab, became the first hospital in the United States to design with safety as its key focus.

I was honored to be CEO of St. Joseph's during that period. The experiences with the National Learning Lab and its effect on design at St. Joseph's changed me and made me dedicated to supporting hospital and health care organizations in using facility design as an opportunity to improve patient safety and enhance or create safety culture.

This book is a "how to" manual, based on my experiences with the National Learning Lab and St. Joseph's Hospital, as well as many hours of additional research, reading, and discussions with many of the world's leaders in the area of safety in health care.

It is my hope that this publication inspires its readers to action, improving the health outcomes and lives of patients receiving care, and the staff who care for them.

John Reiling, M.H.A., M.B.A., Ph.D.
(formerly President and CEO of St. Joseph's Hospital/SynergyHealth, West Bend, WI)

Introduction

Modern hospitals are the cathedrals of the modern era. They are anchors for dynamic civic and financial activity and are extraordinarily complex. In such settings, complexity is manifest not only in the patient and treatment protocols, but also in the interdisciplinary coordination required between providers, the interdependence of humans with technology, the large volumes of information required for decision making, and the residual uncertainty associated with these decisions.

It is widely acknowledged that the physical environment has a significant impact on health and safety; however, hospitals have not been designed with the explicit goal of enhancing patient safety or improved quality through facility design innovations. Despite the recent trend to design patient-centered health care facilities, little assessment of the impact of the built environment on patient outcomes has been conducted amidst the spiraling health care costs. Studies have focused primarily on the effects of light and noise, yet there are many more considerations in facility design that can influence the quality of care such as patient movement, patient visibility, single-patient rooms, and standardization. High staff turnover has also been blamed on the chaotic work environments in most hospitals. Crowded, noisy, poorly thought out nursing stations add to staff stress and increase the risk of medical errors, which, according to the Institute of Medicine's 1999 report, *To Err Is Human*, cause an estimated 98,000 hospitalized deaths in the United States alone. The lack of data available on how the design of health care facilities impacts the quality and safety of patient care inspired me to investigate how design can make a patient's hospital stay a safer, better experience.

It is rare that the opportunity to build a new health care facility emerges; indeed, most hospitals are in a continuous cycle of remodeling and expanding their existing facilities to adapt to changing demands. The United States is in the midst of the largest hospital construction boom in history, with more than 500 hospitals being built with a staggering $200 billion impact.

The traditional hospital design process requires that architects be given program objectives, which are translated into room requirements and followed by the creation of department adjacencies. Once this preliminary information has been provided, room-by-room adjacencies are developed and then a detailed design of each room is completed. Architects then convert room-by-room design to construction blueprints that represent how individuals, equipment, and technology will function together. Equipment and technology planning generally occurs in the later stages of the design process. Typically, no discussion of patient safety or designing around precarious events is raised, creating an opportunity to repeat latent conditions existing in current hospital designs that contribute to active failures (adverse events or sentinel events). Human factors, and the interface and impact of equipment, technology, and facilities are also not typically discussed or explored early in the process.

There is no authoritative guide to designing for safe patient care. Much of the knowledge is proprietary, and lessons learned are not shared. This book will help make these lessons widely available and open to constant improvement.

Contents

Chapter 1 provides an overview of patient safety and the significance of this issue on facility design. This chapter also discusses why humans err and identifies the causes of error within an organization. Mental functioning and conditions that create error are investigated. This chapter establishes the framework for the National Learning Lab and Safety by Design.

Chapter 2 describes the National Learning Lab held in April 2002, providing the background, discussions from the breakout sessions, and the results.

Chapter 3 identifies the recommended activities needed to create the right conditions for a successful safety design. These activities include general design principles; current process review and a description of new safe processes; development of a common belief about the need for safety enhancement; anonymous reporting of medical error, near misses and adverse events; a technology fair; the organization of the design process; and a team approach to design.

Chapter 4 discusses how to apply the safety design process from the National Learning Lab and how to apply the recommendations from the National Learning Lab to eliminate latent conditions and active failures.

Chapter 5 explores how to use the safe facility design process to enhance safety culture, using the recommendations of the National Learning Lab.

Chapter 6 discusses the role of the architect in safe by design, including a new way of thinking as a result of understanding what safety in design is, the impact of a safe design on the traditional design process, and how the architect's culture needs to change to achieve safe designs.

Chapter 7 addresses the importance of physician involvement in the design of a hospital. The chapter explores the historic culture of a physician's independence, autonomy, and perfectionism as an impediment to safety culture and a safe design. It also describes how to develop team behavior and use evidence-based medicine and their impact on design.

Chapter 8 describes how St. Joseph's Hospital in West Bend, Wisconsin, put all the pieces together and successfully designed a new facility around patient safety.

Chapter 9 identifies barriers to safe design and presents strategies to overcome these barriers.

Chapter 10 discusses the significance of the business case for patient safety on safety design.

Acknowledgments

Special thanks to Helen Kline, who has supported my efforts over the past two years to help create this publication.

This publication and the information within it reflect the involvement of SynergyHealth St. Joseph's Hospital in West Bend, Wisconsin, while I was president and CEO there. I would like to acknowledge especially the Chairman of the Board during my tenure, Elaine Shanebrook, who was always thoughtful and supportive; the management staff of St Joseph's who were committed to safety and effectively implementing the Learning Lab recommendations; key medical staff who also contributed to the process, notably Dr. Robert Gibson; and the employees and construction team who made so many contributions. Also thanks to the National Learning Lab participants and other nationally recognized human safety experts, without whose insights and recommendations these safe by design outcomes would not have been possible.

Much of the information contained in this book was documented and developed while I was completing my doctorate at the University of Minnesota. My dissertation committee has continued to encourage me to pursue this book: Ronald S. Hadsall, Ph.D., Sandra J. Potthoff, Ph.D., Jon C. Schommer, Ph.D., and especially my advisor, Theodor J. Litman, Ph.D.

My thanks also go out to Jody Schuman and Lori Milonzi for their assistance throughout this project; and to Cecily Pew and Joint Commission Resources' Department of Publications, for their consistently thorough, professional support.

I am grateful to those individuals, institutions, and organizations that have helped disseminate the safe by design principles outlined in this book, particularly Gary Strack, president and CEO of Boca Raton Community Hospital in Florida, and the entire organization of this hospital for its commitment to fully implementing safe by design principles in their pursuit of becoming the safest teaching hospital in America.

Thanks also to Tom Lynch, a colleague and personal friend, for suggesting the book's title.

My appreciation extends especially to my two colleagues who authored chapters in this book on their areas of professional expertise: John Overton, M.D., who wrote the chapter about physician involvement in safe by design processes; and Tom Wallen, A.I.A., who wrote the chapter on how architects contribute to the principles of safe by design. Their work enhances the value of the book.

I would also like to thank Paul Barach, for his insights and input on this topic.

Finally, to my family: Rob and Kate, my children, for their support; and to Jude, my wife, for her encouragement and commitment—they helped create the conditions so a successful outcome could be reached.

Contributors

John W. Overton Jr., M.D.

With a background in surgery and aviation, Dr. Overton's professional endeavors involve improving safety in health care environments and aeromedical transport.

Dr. Overton obtained his B.S. degree from Virginia Polytechnic Institute and State University and his medical degree from the University of Virginia School of Medicine. He completed his residency training at Emory University and Tufts University and is a Diplomat of the American Boards of Thoracic Surgery, General Surgery and Emergency Medicine.

Dr. Overton practiced cardiothoracic and vascular surgery, and participated as a trauma consultant, at an American College of Surgeons' Level 1 Trauma Program in Minneapolis, for 15 years. He has been a general aviation pilot since 1977 and remains an active pilot.

Dr. Overton has a longstanding interest in safety and process improvement in health care and aviation. In the late 1990s he was a hospital team leader for one of 44 hospitals involved in the Institute for Healthcare Improvement's Breakthrough Series Collaborative on "Improving Outcomes in Adult Cardiac Surgery." He attended the Division of Health Outcomes Research at the University of Minnesota Graduate School of Public Health in 2001.

He is a member of the American Medical Association, the Society of Thoracic Surgeons, and the Air Medical Physicians Association, and he serves as a Board Member for the Commission on Accreditation of Medical Transport Systems.

Dr. Overton's current pursuits consist of consulting in health care safety and participation in a multi-disciplinary alliance of professionals whose focus is just culture, risk and safety management, operational audits, and organizational leadership. As a professional invested in maximizing safety and system efficiency, he acknowledges that there is much to learn and share across disciplines.

Thomas K. Wallen, A.I.A.

Tom Wallen is a leading expert on designing health care environments that improve patient safety by reducing medical error. His design of St. Joseph's Hospital in West Bend, Wisconsin, the revolutionary replacement hospital highly publicized for its radical patient safety initiatives, has been lauded in dozens of publications, including the front page of the *Wall Street Journal*.

Tom's designs enhance safety, flexibility, and operational efficiency while creating aesthetically pleasing and healing environments. His involvement in industry-altering patient safety research and 25 years of architecture experience make him an internationally sought-after speaker.

A principal at Gresham, Smith and Partners, Tom has extended the firm's health care services to clients in Asia. His years of experience as a foreign missionary enable him to connect with clients challenged with improving health care delivery in developing nations.

About Gresham, Smith and Partners:

Gresham, Smith and Partners (GS&P) provides planning, architecture, engineering, and interior design services to national and international clients from 16 offices across the United States. For nearly four decades, GS&P has provided services in multiple markets, including healthcare, corporate and urban design, aviation, civil and land planning, environmental compliance, industrial transportation, and water services. GS&P consistently ranks among the top architectural and engineering firms in the United States.

Chapter 1

An Overview of Patient Safety and Its Impact on Facility Design

"Between the health care we have and the care that we could have lies not just a gap, but a chasm." (Institute of Medicine: *Crossing the Quality Chasm: A New Health System for the 21st Century.* Washington, DC: National Academy Press, 2001, p. 1.)

We are all familiar with the stories of patient harm in health care organizations: Patients being administered the wrong medications or an overdose of their medications, patients having the wrong limb amputated, or patients being mistaken for another patient and receiving the wrong treatment.

Although these cases, and many like them, are horrific, one could argue that they are isolated cases, not indicative of any trend. Lucian Leape referred to this argument when he stated that "the high error rate has not stimulated more concern and effort at prevention. Although error rates are substantial, serious injuries due to errors are perceived as isolated and unusual events, outliers."[1(p.1851)]

The 1998 Institute of Medicine (IOM) National Roundtable on Health Care Quality concluded that serious and widespread quality problems exist throughout American medicine. These problems, which may be classified as underuse, overuse, or misuse, occur in small and large communities alike, in all parts of the country, and with approximately equal frequency in managed care and fee-for-service systems of care. Very large numbers of Americans are harmed as a direct result.[2]

The IOM's 2001 report, *Crossing the Quality Chasm*, sums up well the state of urgency in today's health care industry:

> The American health care delivery system is in need of fundamental change. Many patients, doctors, nurses and health care leaders are concerned that the care delivered is not, essentially, the care we should receive. . . . Health care today harms too frequently and routinely fails to deliver its potential benefits. Americans should be able to count on receiving care that meets their needs and is based on the best scientific knowledge. Yet there is strong evidence that this frequently is not the case. Crucial reports from disciplined review bodies document the scale and gravity of the problems. Quality problems are everywhere, affecting many patients. Between the health care we have and the care that we could have lies not just a gap, but a chasm.[2(p.1)]

The evidence clearly points to the conclusion that patient safety is a serious issue within hospitals in the United States today.

Given the seriousness of patient harm that has occurred in hospitals, many institutions are attempting to enhance patient safety and prevent harm. According to the 1999 IOM report, *To Err Is Human*, improving patient safety means "designing processes of care that lead to less patient harm."

Recommendations from this report include improvement in leadership, reporting systems, and learning culture and implementing safety systems in health care organizations. These safety systems should incorporate safety principles to processes, equipment, and supplies, in areas such as standardization and simplification. The recommendations should also focus on medication errors, suggesting significant process improvements to medication processes such as standardization, physician order entry, patients' knowledge of their treatment, and relevant information at the point of patient care.[4]

Although the designs of organizational processes and systems are being addressed in these recommendations, the impact of facility development on patient safety is not. Is it possible for the design of a hospital facility—including its technology and equipment—to affect the level of patient safety within it? Before answering that question, it is necessary to look at why humans make mistakes in the first place.

Human Error

Humans err. The reason for the sentinel 1999 IOM report *To Err Is Human* was to stress the fact that physicians, caregivers, and in fact the entire human race, all err. What is critical is an understanding of *why* humans err and if facilities, with technology and equipment, can affect human error.

Error and Facility Design: A Connection?

James Reason's[5] and Lucian Leape's[1] model of error, which contends there are conditions that cause interruptions to our neurological system that lead to human error, is widely accepted by health care and other industries. If the conditions causing human error are minimized or eliminated in health care, the result should be less human error, leading to fewer adverse events and preventable medical deaths, improved patient outcomes, and lower costs.

What are the conditions of human error and does a hospital facility, with its equipment and technology, affect them?

In his book *Massive Change,* architect Mau says this about the importance of design:

> For most of us, design is invisible. Until it fails. . . . When systems fail, we become temporarily conscious of the extraordinary force and power of design. Every accident provides a brief moment of awareness of real life, what is actually happening, and our dependence on the underlying systems of design.[6(p.5)]

In *The Challenge of Interior Design,* Kleeman states, "There are those who assert that essentially the design of an interior space and its location not only can communicate with those who enter it but also controls their behavior."[7(p.128)] Norman reports in *The Psychology of Everyday Things* that humans do not always behave clumsily and do not always err, but are much more likely to when things they use are badly conceived and designed.[8] And finally, Moray sums it up by saying that "people of good intention, skilled and experienced, may none the less be forced to commit errors by the way in which the design of their environment calls forth their behavior."[9]

Experts from various fields agree that the physical environment does have a significant impact on safety and human performance. Reason's and Leape's research testifies to the value of practices based on principles that are designed to compensate for human cognitive failings. When applied to the health care field, these principles include, for example, standardization, simplification, and the use of protocols and checklists.[1]

Facilities designed to meet fire safety codes, for instance, impact the health and safety of employees, patients, and families. In "The Role of the Physical Environment in the Hospital for the 21st Century: A Once-in-a-Lifetime Opportunity," Ulrich and Zimring reviewed more than 600 articles and "found rigorous studies that link the physical environment to patient and staff outcomes in four areas:

1. Reduced staff stress and fatigue; increased effectiveness in delivering care
2. Improved patient safety
3. Reduced stress and improved outcomes
4. Improvement in overall health care quality."[10(p.3)]

Human factors analysis, "the study of the interrelationships between humans, the tools they use, and the environment in which they live and work,"[11(p.1484)] is basic to any study of a hospital's design and its effect on the performance of the people who interface with the facility and its fixed and movable equipment and technology. As a result, the design of a facility, with its fixed and movable components, can have a significant impact on human performance.

Human Error and Performance

Human error has been studied for many years by many different professionals. Cognitive psychologists such as James Reason, Jens Rasmussen, Donald Norman, and others have created an accepted theory of why humans err and have learned how to design environments to minimize errors and the harm they can cause. Lucian Leape describes this as "the pathophysiology of error."[4]

Errors are an aberration in normal mental functioning.[1] John Senders stated that the biological reason for error is an interruption of one's neurological system causing a disruption in normal mental functioning.[12] To understand human error, one must first understand normal cognition, our normal thinking processes.

Cognitive Theory

In his summary of the main themes of cognitive theory in the research he reviewed, Reason states that there are two types of mental functioning: One is automatic and unconscious, the other is deliberate and conscious. Automatic and unconscious functions include routine activities that are rapid and effortless, such as brushing our teeth, dressing, driving to work, and many activities at work.[1,13] We can perform these activities, many times in parallel, because we have established knowledge structures in our brain called *schemata*. We have a vast (maybe unlimited) array of these knowledge structures (schemata), forming "an active organization of past reactions," or mental models.[14] These mental models are collections of past experiences that we use to unconsciously perform routine activities.

Common to schemata theory is the idea that schemata contain *informational variables*, or *slots*.[13] Each informational variable or slot only accepts information for current experience consistent with past experience. If current experiences are not consistent with past experiences, we make them fit our mental model, thus creating a biased view of what activities should be performed and how. These schemata are activated by conscious thought or sensory input, such as a horn sounding, temperature, and so on. Once activated, the functioning is automatic, rapid, and effortless.[1] We prefer to operate in the automatic mode whenever possible because less effort is necessary.

The second type of mental functioning is conscious and deliberate. This conscious activity is slow, sequential, and laborious. These activities relate to problem solving, assessments, or observed errors based on unconscious mental functioning. Because people prefer to operate at the unconscious level where they can automatically match to some previous pattern, attempting to consciously calculate or optimize a task is the activity we least prefer.[1,15] It is hard work to think consciously.

A Model of Error

Rasmussen's model of error has become the standard for understanding human error and its relationship to normal cognitive functioning. His model formed the basis for Reason's generic error-modeling system.[16] It is also the model of choice for Norman in *The Psychology of Everyday Things*[8] and Leape in "Error in Medicine."[1]

In Rasmussen's model, human performance is described in three levels. The first level, skill-based, refers to unconscious, schemata-based activities. In the second level, the rule-based level, we try (unconsciously or consciously) to match patterns from previous experiences. Finally, in the third level, the knowledge-based level, we are confronted with novel situations in which we must make use of a slow, laborious, analytical process.[17] We prefer the skill-based level and the (unconscious) rule-based level, and only when these levels do not work do we revert to the conscious, rule-based level or the knowledge-based level. Leape has suggested that experts in any given field have greater schemata, or unconscious mental models; therefore, less conscious functioning (knowledge-based) is necessary.[1] This allows experts to operate at the first or second levels in areas where others (non-experts) would be operating from the slower, knowledge-based level. Errors, then, are either "malfunctioning" schemata at the unconscious level (skill-based or rule-based), or misjudgments at the conscious level (rule-based or knowledge-based).

Skill-based errors usually are called *slips* or *lapses*.[5,16] These are errors to the unconscious cognitive mechanisms (schemata). The plan is correct but the actions fail to go as planned. Therefore, these are errors of execution or execution failures. They are also unintended acts, such as planning to take a book on vacation but leaving it on the counter, forgetting keys when walking out the door, or not remembering a word or event.[13] In health care, examples could be forgetting to call someone to order a treatment or giving a patient the wrong medication.

Rule-based and conscious knowledge-based errors are called *mistakes*. These are errors to the conscious cognitive mechanisms. The plan is incorrect for the circumstance; there is a mismatch between the intention and the outcome. These errors are planning failures and can pass unnoticed for long periods.[5] Another way to view these errors of planning is to consider them problem-solving errors. Examples of such mistakes would be incorrectly diagnosing a patient or incorrectly assessing a patient because of limited training and background. Another instance is properly diagnosing a patient in the emergency department but choosing a poor treatment, one that is not consistent with the best evidence of how to treat the patient's condition. In situations in which one does not have complete or accurate information, it is possible to make poor judgment calls, perhaps generalizing too much. In such cases, the rule (the diagnosis or assessment), might be correct, but its application to the situation stretches the validity of its use. If the tool is a hammer, then the world is a nail.

Knowledge-based errors are often caused by incomplete or inaccurate information, for example giving a patient a drug that he or she is allergic to because the medical record was not accessed when needed. Another type of knowledge-based error can be described as "biased toward overgeneralization." Memory tends to generalize—that is, we see what we think we know or what our past memory generalizes about.[13]

Error, then, is the failure of a planned action to be completed as intended (an error of execution), or the use of an incorrect plan to achieve an aim (an error of planning).[4] Many factors can cause interruptions to our neurological systems, thus leading to skill-based, rule-based, and knowledge-based errors. Examples of personal "interruptions" are multitasking, having too much to do, boredom, fear, stress, anger, fatigue, alcohol, or family problems. Examples of environmental "interruptions" are noise, heat, unusual stimuli, lack of visibility, lack of natural mapping, and other poor design.[1] In addition, lack of complete and accurate information at the point of decision making is a major factor in knowledge-based or problem-solving errors.

Latent Conditions and Active Failures

Recognition that environmental conditions affect human error, coupled with the study of major organizational accidents such as Three Mile Island, Bhopal, and *Challenger*, have led researchers to study the specific impact that organizational factors have on human error. Uncovering their root causes and preventing these accidents from recurring involve more organizational change than personal change. Organizations create the conditions in which the error is likely to occur; therefore, organizations "set up" the individual to fail. In addition, if no change is implemented, the organization's conditions will continue to create the circumstances in which the same errors will occur. Therefore, correcting an organizational issue will have a greater impact on error reduction and safety than focusing on the individuals who erred.[13]

The organizational issues that create the conditions for error are called *latent conditions*. According to Reason, "These latent conditions are adverse consequences which may lie dormant within the system for a long time, only becoming evident when they combine with other factors to breach the system's defenses."[5] Examples of latent conditions are poorly designed facilities, including their technology and equipment, system design issues, training gaps, staff shortages or improper staffing patterns, and poor safety culture. Reason describes these as "blunt end" occurrences.

The errors made by physicians, nurses, pharmacists, and other personnel at the point of service are called *active failures*. Reason describes these as "sharp end" occurrences and their effects are felt almost immediately.[5] Examples include a nurse delivering the wrong medication or a physician performing wrong-site surgery.

Latent conditions are present in all organizations and are usually created by upper management who are responsible for design systems, staffing, policies, and so on. Active failures are committed by employees who are interfacing with patients and the systems or facilities. Active failures happen one at a time, whereas latent conditions can create multiple adverse events. Again, eliminating or minimizing latent conditions has a greater impact on human error than focusing on an individual active failure.

The following example illustrates this concept. Assume that one person in the country has control over speed limits. This person increases the speed limit to 50 m.p.h. in residential neighborhoods so that working parents can get home faster to be with their families. The effect of this decision (a latent condition) is an increase in deaths and injury to those driving in the neighborhood and those living in the neighborhood. When a driver, "set up" by the policy to drive 50 m.p.h., harms a child, society chastises the driver, trains him or her to be more vigilant, perhaps calling him or her reckless, and possibly demands incarceration. This effort at the "sharp end" may not lower the rising injury rate, but reducing the speed limit to 25 or 30 m.p.h. at the "blunt end" would change the latent condition and thus reduce injuries.

A Safety Model

In *Managing the Risks of Organizational Accidents*, Reason developed a model of safety and error reduction, as shown in Figure 1-1 (page 7).

Hazards are inherent in health care as with any complex organization. Defenses could include technology, equipment, well-designed facilities, systems with standardized protocol, or human checks of a process. The more complicated or linked (tightly coupled) the defenses are, the more likely the defenses will fail.[18]

In most processes in health care, multiple defenses exist. For example, most medication systems have multiple checks: A physician orders, a nurse checks, a pharmacist checks, and a nurse checks again. Potential errors that could result in the wrong drug being delivered to the patient are identified at one of the checkpoints. This way of catching an error before it causes harm is defined as a *near miss* (*see* Figure 1-2 on page 7).

Errors periodically escape all the defense checks, resulting in an active failure called an *adverse event* (*see* Figure 1-3, page 8). Too often, the person involved in the active failure is blamed. For example, the person delivering the drug at the sharp end, the last defense, is blamed, while the cause could or probably does include the failed defenses upstream at the "blunt end."

Active failures and adverse events (that is, harm) occur because the defenses are not as robust as they could be. They are fallible, thus allowing harm to occur as a result of either active failures or latent conditions. Examples of latent conditions are noise, fatigue, poor facilities with their equipment and technology, lack of standardization, and inadequate policies, all of which can help make "Swiss cheese holes" (*see* Figure 1-4 on page 8). These "holes" also could come from individual/team action cognitive failures (active failures). Figure 1-5 (page 9) brings together the various causes of error, showing how they can penetrate defenses to cause error. This model also illustrates how lessening latent conditions and active failures would lower error rates that lead to patient harm, thus raising the level of patient

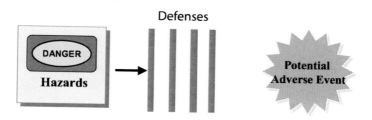

**Hazards are inherent in health care—it's part of "the business."
Defenses can be hardware (e.g., monitors), people (e.g., nurses),
or administrative (e.g., acceptable protocols)**

(From *Managing the Risks of Organizational Accidents*, Reason, 1997)

Figure 1-1. A Generic Model of Safety.
This figure illustrates how defenses are in place to block hazards from harming patients.

Source: Adapted by John Wreathall, from Reason J.: *Managing the Risks of Organizational Accidents.*
Aldershot, UK: Ashgate Publishing, 1997. Used with permission.

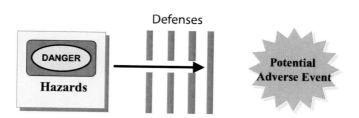

**Usually several defenses must fail to cause an accident—
Just one remaining intact is enough to prevent a near
miss becoming an accident . . .**

Figure 1-2. A Near Miss.
This figure shows that all defenses but one have failed. The remaining defense has prevented a potential hazard from penetrating that defense, thus blocking an adverse event from occurring.

Source: Adapted by John Wreathall, from Reason J.: *Managing the Risks of Organizational Accidents.*
Aldershot, UK: Ashgate Publishing, 1997. Used with permission.

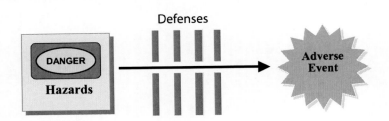

What is "the cause"? The hazard? Failure of which defense?
This is the problem with assigning single causes . . .
Blame/cause often is assigned to the last barrier—usually a
person—to fail!!

Figure 1-3. A Harmful Event.
This figure shows that an adverse event has occurred because a hazard has penetrated all defenses.

Source: Adapted by John Wreathall, from Reason J.: *Managing the Risks of Organizational Accidents.* Aldershot, UK: Ashgate Publishing, 1997. Used with permission.

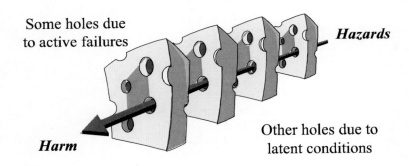

Figure 1-4. The "Swiss Cheese" Model of Safety.
In this figure, each piece of cheese represents a barrier to harm. When the barriers (represented by a hole in the cheese) fail, harm happens.

Source: Adapted by John Wreathall, from Reason J.: *Managing the Risks of Organizational Accidents.* Aldershot, UK: Ashgate Publishing, 1997. Used with permission.

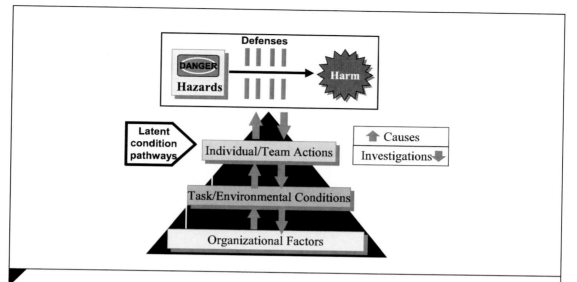

Figure 1-5. Causes of Errors.
This model asks the question, "Why aren't the barriers robust enough to stop the errors from occurring?" The answer lies in the "latent condition pathways" shown.

Source: Adapted by John Wreathall, from Reason J.: *Managing the Risks of Organizational Accidents.* Aldershot, UK: Ashgate Publishing, 1997. Used with permission.

safety. As Norman states, "My research activities led me to the study of human error and industrial accidents. I began to realize that human error resulted from bad design. Humans did not always behave so clumsily. But they do so when the things they do are badly conceived, badly designed."[8(p.42)]

By improving human factors[11] through facility design and ensuring that facility design minimizes the latent conditions and cognitive failures that lead to adverse events, patient safety[19] will be enhanced. This means developing a strong safety culture, redesigning systems or facilities with their equipment and technology, focusing on eliminating the conditions of cognitive errors, or helping caregivers correct an error before it leads to harm.

A Birth: The National Learning Lab

From an initial awareness that patient safety is a serious problem in hospitals, integrated with a model of human error, and inspired by *To Err Is Human*, grew a desire to make patient safety a part of a hospital's facility design, including its equipment and technology. As a result, the National Learning Lab was born. Conducted in Milwaukee, Wisconsin, in April 2002 and sponsored by SynergyHealth St. Joseph's Hospital in West Bend and in part by the University of Minnesota's Program in Health Care Administration, the National Learning Lab set a goal of creating the definitions and road map for safety by design, including safe design principles, process recommendations, and an enhanced safety culture using facility design. The National Learning Lab thus created an opportunity for organizations to follow its recommendations. The participants were committed to disseminating the lab's findings, because they felt the lessons they learned should be shared, leading to increased use of patient safe design principles in hospitals of the future. As a result, the findings of the National Learning Lab have sparked the interest of hospitals, both nationally and internationally, to implement these safety-by-design principles in their individual contexts. The next chapter discuss the National Learning Lab in more detail.

References

1.   Leape L.L.: Error in medicine. *JAMA* 272(23):1851–1857, 1994.

2.   Chassin M.R., Galvin R.W., and the Institute of Medicine National Roundtable on Health Care Quality (A Consensus Statement): The urgent need to improve health care quality. *JAMA* 280(11):1000–1005, 1998.

3.   Institute of Medicine: *Crossing the Quality Chasm: A New Health System for the 21st Century.* Washington, DC: National Academy Press, 2001.

4.   Institute of Medicine: *To Err Is Human: Building a Safer Health System.* Washington, DC: National Academy Press, 1999.

5.   Reason J.: *Managing the Risks of Organizational Accidents.* Aldershot, UK: Ashgate Publishing, 1997.

6.   Mau B.: *Massive Change.* London: Phaidon Press, 2004.

7.   Kleeman W.B. Jr.: *The Challenge of Interior Design.* New York: Van Nostrand Reinhold, 1983.

8.   Norman D.A.: *The Psychology of Everyday Things.* New York: Basic Books, 1988.

9.   Moray N.: Error reduction as a systems problem. In Bogner M.S. (ed.): *Human Error in Medicine.* Boca Raton, FL: CRC Press, 1994, pp. 67–91.

10.   Ulrich R., Zimring C.: The role of the physical environment in the hospital of the 21st century: A once-in-a-lifetime opportunity. Report to The Center for Health Design, for the Designing for the 21st Century Hospital Project, 2004.

11.   Weinger M.B.: Incorporating human factors into the design of medical devices. *JAMA* 280(17):1484, 1998.

12.   Personal communication between the author and John Senders, Clambake 3 Conference, Chicago, September 19–20, 2002. Reason, in *Human Error,* cites John Senders, organizer of Clambake 1, the first Human Error Conference at Columbia Falls, Maine, in 1980, as "one of the great impresarios of human error."

13.   Reason J: *Human Error.* New York: Cambridge University Press, 1990.

14.   Bartlett F.C.: *Remembering: A Study in Experimental and Social Psychology.* Cambridge: Cambridge University Press, 1932.

15.   Rouse W.B.: Models of human problem solving: Detection, diagnosis and compensation for system failures. In *Proceedings of IFAC Conference on Analysis, Design and Evaluation of Man-Machine Systems.* Baden-Baden, FRG: September 1981.

16.   Rasmussen J.: Skills, rules, knowledge: Signals, signs, and symbols and other distinctions in human performance models. Institute of Electrical and Electronics Engineers: *Transactions on Systems, Man & Cybernetics* SMC-13(3):257–266, 1983. *See also* Institute of Medicine, 1999, p. 198.

17.   Rasmussen J., Jensen A.: Mental procedures in real-life tasks: A case study of electronic troubleshooting. *Ergonomics* 17(3):293–307, 1974.

18.   Perrow C.: *Normal accidents: Living with High-Risk Technologies.* New York: Basic Books, 1984.

19.   National Patient Safety Foundation: NPSF announces patient safety research and development agenda. *Focus on Patient Safety* 2(4):1, 1999.

Chapter 2
The National Learning Lab

"The American health care delivery system is in need of fundamental change. . . . Health care today harms too frequently and routinely fails to deliver its potential benefits." (Institute of Medicine: *Crossing the Quality Chasm: A New Health System for the 21st Century.* Washington, DC: National Academy Press, 2001, p. 1.)

Many factors led to the formation of the National Learning Lab in April 2002. As early as 1978, Mills had published his study documenting the significance of safety issues in hospitals.[1] Then in 1999, the Institute of Medicine (IOM) published *To Err Is Human: Building a Safer Health System,* which did much to raise awareness about the preventable harm that was happening to patients in hospitals, despite the rapid increase in life-saving and life-extending technologies and procedures. The issue of patient safety began to catch on as hospitals, hospital caregivers, patients, and related businesses began examining how to improve the "safety quotient" of hospital system design.

Could the design of a new hospital, with its technology and equipment, be planned to optimize patient safety? This intriguing question eventually led to the formation of a National Learning Lab to explore the issue of hospital safety design. The purpose of the lab was to define and create a road map for safety by design, including safe design principles, process recommendations, and an enhanced safety culture for hospitals through facility design focused on patient safety. Its five planning suggestions included the following:

1. Discuss the major errors occurring at St. Joseph's, as compared to a manufacturing company, where, if a product with quality problems was discovered, the root causes were researched and change was implemented to the process, the facility, the equipment, or the technology, to correct the problem.
2. Identify general design principles for hospital safety.
3. Focus on changes to the facility design process, moving from the traditional to more safety-conscious processes.
4. Explore the impact of new design principles on safety culture.
5. Learn from the aviation industry and from the safety models of James Reason and Lucian Leape, as expressed in *To Err Is Human: Building a Safer Health System.*

Key speakers included John Wreathall, M.Sc., who presented James Reason's model of accident prevention and safety and discussed designing safe facilities, using his experience with nuclear power and transportation issues; Donald Holmquest, M.D., Ph.D., J.D., a physician, scientist, and astronaut previously with NASA, who reflected on the spaceflight/aviation industry and what lessons from aviation safety could be applied to health care, specifically patient safety and facility development; and John Reiling, M.H.A., M.B.A., Ph.D., president/CEO of SynergyHealth, Inc., and St. Joseph's Hospital, who discussed the concept of facility-driven system changes to improve safety, reinforcing the underlying need and value of working toward improved patient safety.

The key speakers offered insights not only from health care, but also from other industries and fields of expertise, as they and the conference participants examined the complex, tightly coupled health care industry for ways to improve patient safety. Hospitals are labor intensive and capital intensive. Significant clinical technology changes occur rapidly, and equipment changes also add to the complexity, while at the same time offering patients the potential for improved treatment and outcomes. Patients who are vulnerable receive an enormous range of services that are intrinsic to medicine and health care delivery. It is useful to note that the patient, the ultimate customer, is judging the service as he or she receives the service, as compared to most industries in which the point of production (service) is different from the point of sale (customer service).

The conference participants included representatives from many of the organizations involved in the patient safety movement, many of whom sent their top leadership, including the following:

American Hospital Association
American Medical Association
American Pharmaceutical Association
American Society for Quality
Department of Veterans Affairs, Midwest Center for Patient Safety
Institute for Healthcare Improvement
Institute for Safe Medication Practices
Joint Commission on Accreditation of Healthcare Organizations (The Joint Commission)
Medical Group Management Association
National Patient Safety Foundation
Patient Safety Institute
University of Minnesota
University of Wisconsin–Milwaukee
Veterans Healthcare Administration
Wisconsin Hospital Association

In addition, representatives of the design team (architects, contractors, mechanical, electrical, plumbing, engineering, owner's representative) and medical staff leadership from St. Joseph's participated. Board members, physicians, community members, management leadership, nurses, pharmacists, and other caregivers observed the proceedings.

Human Error and Safety Culture

Wreathall presented James Reason's model of safety, addressing principles learned from other industries and applying them to hospital facility design and safety, as seen in Figure 1-5 on page 9.

Usually in health care, several defenses must fail for a harmful event to occur. If one defense stops the hazard, the harm is prevented (*near miss*). Most often a series of failed events (*defenses*) lead to a final defense failure; many of this series of failed events require human involvement. Typically the person at the final barrier is blamed for the harm (*active failure*). Wreathall illustrated how defenses against harm are fallible (as are humans), with holes in each level of defense (the Swiss Cheese Model described in

Figure 1-4 on page 8). These weaknesses in defense can be termed either *active failures* or *latent conditions*. *Active failures*, such as forgetting to check a medication before giving it or reviewing the medication but not actually seeing the error, typically occur at the point of harm (*adverse events*). *Latent conditions*, such as poor lighting, poor departmental adjacencies, other facility design features, and organizational factors, can lay dormant, at times unnoticed, creating weaknesses in the system.

Most harm is the result of an individual action. But deeper analysis into the cause of adverse events identifies the work environment as creating the conditions or influencing the likelihood of unsafe acts. Organizational factors such as staffing levels, policies, and safety culture systems shape the work environment, leading to safe or unsafe acts. Therefore, hospital facilities with their technology and equipment do impact individual and organizational performance.

Other high-risk industries, such as commercial aviation and nuclear power (*see* Figure 2-1, below, and Figure 2-2 on page 14), have achieved high levels of safety using Reason's model of safety.

Wreathall emphasized that by recognizing the relationship between facility design and organization on the one hand and environmental conditions and individual/team actions (both latent conditions and active failures) on the other, people will understand what drives safety risk and safety. This understanding can then help design a safe hospital. Tools such as failure mode and effects analysis (FMEA) can help identify safety risks. FMEA will be discussed in detail in Chapter 4.

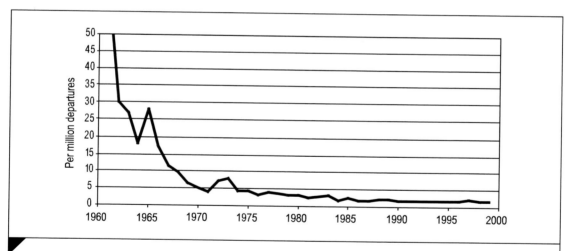

Figure 2-1. Commercial Aviation Accident Rate.
In this figure, the vertical axis of the graph represents the number of commercial airplane accidents per million departures worldwide; the horizontal axis lists years; clearly the rate of accidents has dropped sharply from the 1960s to 2000. Source for data: Statistical Summary of Commercial Jet Airplane Accidents Worldwide Operations 1959–1999. Seattle, WA, Boeing Commercial Airplane Group.

Source: John Wreathall, National Learning Lab presentation, Milwaukee, WI: 2002. Used with permission.

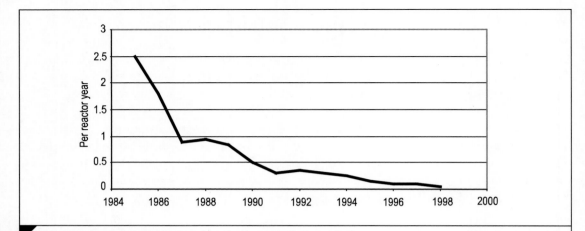

Figure 2-2. Nuclear Power Plants' Significant Event Rate.
This figure shows that the rate of significant accidents in nuclear plants in the United States dropped sharply from the 1960s to 2000. Source for data: The NRC Annual Report, 1999 (NUREG-1145, Vol. 15). Rockville, MD, U.S. Nuclear Regulatory Commission.

Source: John Wreathall, National Learning Lab presentation, Milwaukee, WI: 2002. Used with permission.

Safety culture—including the concepts of a just culture, a reporting culture, and a learning culture—can all be affected by facilities, where physical systems, administration, and safety culture all come together and impact safe performance. Designing to create a safe environment demands that an organization understand the errors occurring and learn how to design them out. Facility design can set the framework for creating or enhancing values. By focusing on structures that impact safety (and considering active failures and latent conditions), a culture of safety will be created or enhanced. A safety culture should be engineered *intentionally* into the facility design process.

Spaceflight Aviation: Risk Awareness

During his presentation, Holmquest underscored the fact that failures in patient safety in hospitals are usually organizational and system failures that "set up" individuals for failure. In building safe hospitals, professionals must be keenly aware of the enormous risks that exist with highly complex patient care tools and processes. In Holmquest's opinion, spacecraft design for crew safety is easier than hospital design for patient safety. Professionals and the public are much more aware of the risks involved with aviation and space travel than with hospitalization. This awareness results in a culture of safety in the space and airline industries that is not present in health care.

The hazards of spaceflight environment are obvious: height, high speed, lack of oxygen, extreme temperature, remoteness, and difficulty of rescue. As a result, there is a need for total life support, including oxygen, water, light, pressure, temperature, and radiation. When errors occur, the consequences are dramatic, shocking, and forever remembered. The dramatic results enhance the corrective response and the determination to fix the problem.

In hospitals, the hazards are not so obvious, even to professionals. No fast flight, no extreme temperatures, no need for changes in atmospheric pressure, no remote off-world locations, no life support necessary (except during certain circumstances such as surgery). Nor do patients usually die in large groups. Instead, a single patient dies, sometimes alone during the night, sometimes while being attended by multiple professionals. In fact, it is expected that a certain number of patients in hospitals will die, typically the result of an illness that caused the patient's admission. When patients die, death is attributed to natural causes or just bad luck. Every death is investigated as to cause, but the most obvious, or simplest, cause is likely the one identified. Risk managers often become managers of litigation risk, not promoters of patient safety.

When an aviation crew dies, the mission is a total failure. Investigations, hearings, and reports follow. Figure 2-3 points out that when patients die in hospitals, life in the hospital tends to go on as before; developing a "fault-free environment" is typically not part of the hospital's "mission."

Holmquest stated that in hospital design, patients and even caregivers are not typically part of the design process. Architects traditionally present their view of design with input from management leadership but without much input from the caregivers and patients. In spacecraft design, even though spacecraft engineers and architects begin the design process, astronauts are actively and explicitly involved with the design process. Spacecraft design emphasizes functionality and safety. Hospital design emphasizes structure and aesthetics, and safety is secondary to appearance.

Holmquest then made a final set of comparisons between aviation and health care. In aviation, design mock-ups by the end user are an explicit and ongoing part of design. Architects and engineers perform original design, but the end user tests and redesigns repeatedly to ensure that safe design has been achieved. For example, creating a standardized "stowage list" for all astronauts involved years of design by astronauts, architects, and engineers. Every potential failure that was identified was designed out if at all possible. As such, patient safety must be as much a part of the objective of hospital facility design as crew safety is for NASA missions.

• When the crew dies, the mission is a total failure.	• When patients die, life tends to go on fairly normally.
• Investigations, hearings, reports, and accountability follow. (Where is North American Rockwell today?)	• A fault-free environment is typically not part of the hospital "mission."

Figure 2-3. Errors and Consequences.
This figure shows the contrast between the consequences of failure in a space mission and in a hospital setting.

Source: Donald Holmquest, National Learning Lab presentation. Milwaukee, WI: 2002. Used with permission.

Holmquest pointed out that the application of technology in aviation has been one of its most important tools in improving safety and lowering the number of deaths. Hospitals and spacecraft are similar in that both are complex facilities in which the whole purpose is to complete complex processes over and over again without error. This means each defense has to be designed for an extremely high level of accuracy so that the resulting outcome has a high likelihood of success.

Facility infrastructure must be designed to support or facilitate the defenses and processes and help eliminate the holes in these defenses. In aviation, the processes are standardized as much as possible and applied consistently. For example, a standardized checklist is used before every flight. Hospitals need to instill the same rigor. Standardization, the use of information systems, and technology to automate communication and provide decision support should be critical parts of safe facility design.

Holmquest reemphasized that there are enormous risks in hospitals, risks that daily cause significant harm, due in part to highly complex equipment and processes. He recommended focusing everyone's skills on designing an environment that facilitates the use of systematic process consistently applied. The goal should be the safety of every single subject, whether caregiver or patient.

Safe Hospital Design

During his presentation, Reiling emphasized that hospital design can be improved to positively affect processes, care delivery, and management culture. Using data from the IOM's 1999 study, *To Err Is Human*, Reiling underscored the need for making hospitals safer. Put simply, the high number of preventable deaths in hospitals in the United States today is unacceptable.

Hospitals exist to care for people, not to cause harm or have them die from a preventable condition. Furthermore, the costs of harm are extraordinary, estimated to be between $17 billion and $29 billion a year—of which health care–related costs represent more than one-half.[2] Reiling emphasized that this is the reason why a focus on patient safety in design is the *right* thing to do. It should be a mandate for the future.

Many health care providers—physicians, nurses, pharmacists—live with the knowledge that they have harmed a patient. They may have been taught to equate these human errors with incompetence, as in the "medical model," in which perfection is competence and human error is incompetence. This belief leads to guilt and shame. It is hospital leadership's responsibility to create conditions in which the possibility for human error can be detected before it happens, or at the very least minimized, and caregivers are allowed to recover from the error. This should be accomplished through safe facility design, process redesign, and development of a safety culture that puts providers in a position to succeed. Hospitals need to stop "setting up" people to fail.

To design facilities focused on safety demands, health care needs to change the way a facility is traditionally designed. The facility features, including technology and equipment, need to change to eliminate the active failures and latent conditions that lead to harm. Finally, the facility design process needs to change to enhance or create a safety culture. "We cannot change the human condition, but we can change the conditions under which people work."[3(p.25)]

Participant Discussion Groups

The conference participants were given four tasks:

1. Develop recommendations to improve the traditional design process to make it more patient safety focused.
2. List general patient safety design principles, including general patient safety principles around technology and equipment.
3. Provide recommendations around adverse events. These were identified with input from The Joint Commission and the Department of Veterans Affairs National Center for Patient Safety.
4. Define a patient safety culture and assess whether the design of facilities with their technology and equipment could create or enhance a patient safety culture.

The conference participants then analyzed the speakers' ideas and reviewed the traditional facility design process, shown in Table 2-1 (below). Their task was to reconsider the traditional facility design process in light of the information presented during the opening session, and to generate guidelines and recommendations to modify the traditional process driven by the commitment to patient safety (*see* Table 2-2, below).

The participants also considered what general design principles should be used for creating a safe facility, focusing on latent conditions (*see* Table 2-3, page 18) that have been historically designed into facilities. The participants discussed how technology could lower latent conditions and harm as well as the complexities that equipment and technology bring to hospitals. General conditions that lead to error, such as noise and fatigue, were explored and principles were developed.

The groups then made facility design recommendations focused on 10 specific types of hospital-adverse

Table 2-1. Steps in the Traditional Facility Design Process
Role and program
Functional space programming
Adjacencies (block diagrams)
Schematic design
Design development
Construction documents
Construction

Table 2-2. Safety Design Process Recommendations
1. Matrix development (postlearning lab)
2. FMEA at each stage of design
3. Patients/families involved in design process
4. Equipment planning from Day 1
5. Mock-ups from Day 1
6. Design for the vulnerable patient
7. Articulation of a set of principles for measurement
8. Establishment of a checklist for current/future design

Table 2-3. Latent Conditions	Table 2-4. Active Failures
1. Noise reduction	1. Operative/postop complications/infections
2. Scalability, adaptability, flexibility	2. Inpatient suicides
3. Visibility of patients to staff	3. Incorrect tube—incorrect connector—incorrect hole placement events
4. Patients involved with their care	4. Medication error–related events
5. Standardization	5. Wrong-site surgery events
6. Automation where possible	6. Oxygen cylinder hazards
7. Minimizing fatigue	7. Deaths of patients in restraints
8. Immediate accessibility of information, close to the point of service	8. Transfusion-related events
9. Minimizing patient transfers/hand offs	9. Patient falls
	10. MRI hazards

events and their root causes (*see* Table 2-4, above) that had been identified earlier through a review of the Joint Commission's Sentinel Events database and input from the Department of Veterans Affairs.

One breakout group specifically defined safety culture and ways of using the facility design process focused on patient safety to enhance or create safety culture. Other breakout groups made safety culture recommendations (*see* Table 2-5 page 19).

Finally, after each group presented its work, the top 10 recommendations from all participants were presented, as shown in Table 2-6, page 19.

It is interesting to note that many of these recommendations, such as 1, 4, 9, and 10, are related to safety design process recommendations. A few of the top 10 were latent condition strategies, such as 6 (noise reduction) and 2 (standardization). No specific precarious events or active failures listed in Table 2-4 or any of the safety culture recommendations listed in Table 2-5 made it to the list in Table 2-6. Participants believed that a facility design process should focus on patient safety and that addressing the top 10 issues would also address all latent conditions, active failures, and safety culture recommendations.

After the Learning Lab ended, the next step was for hospitals everywhere to begin using the National Learning Lab recommendations to enhance patient safety through facility design, with its equipment and technology.

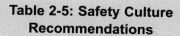

Table 2-5: Safety Culture Recommendations

1. Shared values and beliefs about safety within the organization
2. Always anticipating precarious events
3. Informed employees and medical staff
4. Culture of reporting
5. Learning culture
6. "Just" culture
7. Blame-free environment recognizing human fallibility
8. Physician teamwork
9. Culture of continuous improvement
10. Empowering families to participate in care of patients
11. Informed and active patients

Table 2-6. Top Ten Recommendations

1. Conduct FMEA at each stage of design.
2. Standardize location of equipment, supplies, room layout, and care processes.
3. Involve patients/families in the design process.
4. Use an established checklist for current/future design.
5. Bring critical information that is used for decision-making close to the patient.
6. Reduce noise.
7. Use adaptive systems that will allow function in the future.
8. Articulate a set of principles by which everything is measured.
9. Begin equipment planning from Day 1.
10. Begin mock-ups on Day 1.

References

1. Mills D.H.: Medical Insurance Feasibility Study—A technical summary. *Western Journal of Medicine* 128(4):360–365, 1978.
2. Institute of Medicine: *To Err Is Human: Building a Safer Health System.* Washington, DC: National Academy Press, 1999.
3. Reason J.: *Managing the Risks of Organizational Accidents.* Aldershot, UK: Ashgate Publishing, 1997.

Chapter 3
Preparing for the Facility Safety Design Process

"We cannot change the human condition, but we can change the conditions under which people work."
(James Reason, *Managing the Risks of Organizational Accidents*. Aldershot, UK: Ashgate Publishing, 1997, p. 25.)

This chapter outlines the various ways a health care organization can prepare for a facility design process focused on safety. Historically in the design process, architects who create plans to replicate current organizational processes and previous room design are engaged. However, enhancing safety demands that current processes are reviewed and changed to create conditions in which caregivers and those who support them can succeed. Design that uses current processes will result only in the same level of harm that currently exists. One cannot expect to use the same process and have different results. Therefore, the traditional facility design process needs to be modified to focus on safety.

General Design Principles

As a health care organization prepares to focus on a patient-safe facility design, participants in the planning process need a new mind-set, that is, a new way of thinking about facility design and how to prepare the organization for the changes to come.

As a first step, ask your organization's major stakeholders to identify their expectations of the facility project's outcome. During this interchange, educate the stakeholders on the importance of safety in design, including its definition, background, and the National Learning Lab recommendations. The list below outlines examples of the type of values, or principles, that a patient-safe facility will exemplify:

1. *Patient Centered.* The hospital will be designed to meet the patient's physical, emotional, and spiritual needs and respect each patient's dignity and privacy.
2. *Environmentally Healthful.* Beauty, quiet, nature, light, and peace will create an atmosphere conducive to healing and comfort in this facility.
3. *Efficient.* The hospital will be designed to make the movement of people, services, and supplies easy and efficient now and in the future.
4. *Safe.* The hospital will be designed to create error-free systems and a culture of safety for the protection of the patients and staff.
5. *Quality Care.* High-quality care will be ensured by providing an environment that fosters clinical excellence through systems, technology, and a culture of safety.
6. *Technologically Advanced.* A wide range of information, resources, and technology will be provided to develop service lines that promote high-quality patient care in the hospital and in the community.
7. *Staff Friendly.* The hospital will be known as a place where people are proud and happy to work, where employees and their families are valued, and where opportunities for learning and personal growth are encouraged.

Your organization's completed project should exhibit the principles that your organization's stakeholders have agreed upon.

Strategies That Support a Safety Design Process

The challenge for any hospital or health care organization is to evolve from the traditional design process to a new process that focuses on patient safety, using the process design recommendations developed by the National Learning Lab (*see* Chapter 4). One of the first steps is to initiate a culture change, one that supports the new design process. The following sections outline some of the strategies and procedures that facilitate such a culture change.

Common Belief and Anonymous Reporting

The National Learning Lab created an invigorating atmosphere, as people were changed by observing or participating in it. They realized the enormity of the patient safety issue in health care and the unique opportunity they had to use the facility development process—including technology and equipment—to affect it.

Yet one of the first roadblocks to facilitating a patient safety environment is getting staff comfortable with acknowledging—and ultimately reporting—errors. The current reporting system and incident reports common in most hospitals in the United States lead some to believe in a "that doesn't happen in our hospital" mentality. The caregivers at most hospitals are trained with the belief that competence means perfection and incompetence is related to error. For example, a nurse giving the wrong medication is the result of a lack of vigilance, and possibly incompetence.

This culture of "blame and shame" minimizes error reporting. A caregiver who makes a *human* error (that is, a lapse or mistake) would be less likely to report it because he or she knows the consequences—having the error added to his or her personnel record or reported to the Quality Committee or administration. This could lead to suspension, termination, and/or public reporting to state and federal agencies.

Another concern employees and physicians have is how to eliminate adverse events if (they believe) those problems are not present in the first place. These adverse events and errors might be prevalent in other hospitals, but not at one's own institution. "Show me" is often the attitude: Why should our organization design around minimizing medication errors, near misses, adverse events, and the conditions that cause them if they are not happening here?

One way to begin developing a reporting culture is to create an anonymous reporting system that includes streamlining any existing incident reporting process, such as allowing employees to report incidents to a neutral third party, such as an accounting firm. Doing this can help alleviate concerns about possible consequences for reported errors. The reporting period can be short (for example, two weeks) to encourage a higher number of reports.

Questions that could be asked in an anonymous reporting survey include the following:

1. If you know of any medical errors that have occurred, please describe what you have observed. If you know any "near misses" that have occurred, please describe.
2. If you know of any unsafe conditions/processes that exist, please describe.
3. Can you think of anything that can be done through physical design, equipment, technology, or systems that could prevent medical errors from happening in the future?

This exercise can spark the development or enhancement of a hospital's ongoing reporting system. An ongoing reporting system is essential for improving safety and quality in an organization, because it allows one to see the risks and adverse events that lead to harm.

In addition to the anonymous reporting system, storytelling—having staff share stories about incidents they have observed or been part of in the hospital—can be encouraged so that employees can learn from each other. Staff can also watch videotapes of people from other organizations describing problematic incidents. Watching the tapes and sharing stories with others can help raise awareness of safety issues. When people are more aware of problems and how others deal with them, their commitment to safety in design increases. In addition, sharing the results of the reporting, which enhances the process of becoming transparent, is an essential tool to creating a common belief around safety.

The results of the storytelling and the anonymous reporting system can begin to change the culture within a hospital and help staff develop shared values and beliefs about safety within the organization.

Use of Technology

Many participants at the National Learning Lab believed that technology could have a material impact on latent conditions and active failures. For example, using a nurse call system that has vibration capability to eliminate overhead paging could lower the impact of noise. Computerized prescriber order entry and bar coding could lower the number of medication errors. In fact, some of the recommendations to minimize active failures have significant technology solutions.

Hospitals should be aware of all the technological possibilities in health care (such as wireless phones, nurse call systems, a pneumatic tube system, bar coding, radio frequency identification devices, telephones, cabling, integrated information systems, best-of-breed software systems, robots, and PACS [Picture Archiving and Communication System] image transfer) and the capital necessary to acquire them. A technology fair in which multiple vendors visit the hospital to demonstrate the latest technology is one way to expose the hospital to potential technologies that would impact safety and ensure quality. To maximize safety in design, an organization must balance technology with fixed and movable equipment and its physical plant. An organization doesn't have to have the capital for all its proposed technology at once. The organization can at least plan the infrastructure and install it initially so that future technologies can be added as the monies become available.

Review of Core Processes

Before their involvement in the design process, most health care architectural firms collect data from individual departments and the entire organization on volumes of services, key processes, requested adjacencies, the number of employees, the hours of operations, key technologies, or contemplated key services. Historically, architects use these data to determine how many rooms, by functional type, are needed, what the departmental areas are, and then how to arrange rooms within a department. As part of the data collection process, current processes are usually described. Many facilities take existing processes (ways of performing functions) and expect the new facility to be designed to continue those processes in the same ways. This allows latent conditions and active failures that lead to adverse events to be redesigned into the new construction. Furthermore, because many processes in a hospital involve multiple departments, data collected by any single department might not reflect the needs of all departments involved with the process.

Based on recommendations from the National Learning Lab, in the new facility design process an institution can start designing anew. Processes can be new, redesigned, or status quo. A hospital can ask: Is the way we are performing functions today the way we want to perform them tomorrow? Should processes be changed or created to encourage safety and meet the design principles? Before the architects arrive, teams can be formed to brainstorm and design idealized core processes, which could include the following:

- Medication
- Admitting/Discharge
- Diagnostics
- Patient Care Service Delivery
- Supply Handling/Delivery/Waste Removal
- Transportation and Movement Documentations
- Scheduling
- Medical Staff Processes/Needs
- Financial Processes
- Women's Services
- Medical Education
- Heart Patients
- Cancer Patients
- Surgery
- Emergency Room
- Other Centers of Excellence

When core process teams start meeting, the subsequent discussions are likely to be uplifting yet difficult. They can be uplifting because employees can envision different ways of performing processes to meet the design principles; they are likely to be difficult where change is hard to internalize. Some people will be invested in the known, familiar processes and will therefore resist change. However, members of the core process teams can find the brainstorming process a helpful approach to challenge thinking about processes that are focused on safety function.

A Team Approach to Design

Most hospital facility design processes have an internal Steering Committee that interfaces with the external design team (architects, contractors, and others) to oversee the design process. Members of the Steering Committee typically include organization leadership, such as the president, the chief operating officer, and the vice president of Patient Care Services. When schematics and design development stages are conducted, department managers and potentially others (departmental employees) are involved in translating the departmental block diagrams into department-based adjacencies (schematic) and detailed room drawings (design development).

The weakness of this organizational structure is that while a small number of physicians are typically invited to join, front-line employees and patients and their families are not. Safe facility design should help employees who are providing care (the front-line employees), as well as most physicians, work in an environment where the risk of error is minimized, not in an environment where they are set up for failure. To accomplish this, the human factors of employees need to be understood. The daily and minute-to-minute interface of employees with the process and the facility is what a safety design should address. The best source for this information and input is the employees. Another way to get employees and physicians involved in safety design is to invite them to participate in mock-ups (*see* page 45 in Chapter 4).

One way to obtain this feedback is to hold retreats or focus groups with front-line employees and patients and their families. Another way is to create committees (in addition to the Steering Committee) of front-line employees, patients, their families, and physicians. A physician advisory committee could also be useful for getting physicians more actively involved. All these committees could be used to filter ideas to the Steering Committee. Front-line employees can help ensure that safety design principles are being met across departments. Input from patients and their families is also crucial and should be forwarded to design teams. Practicing physicians can also help ensure that these principles are being met across departments.

Hundreds of employees, physicians, and community members typically participate in a health care organization. One of the benefits that results from so many participants working together is that reporting of near misses, errors, and adverse events may dramatically increase during the design period. Overall, team effort changes the culture and improves the safety design of a hospital.

The Similarities of the National Learning Lab Recommendations and Quality Improvement Methodologies

Many approaches have been used in health care to create or enhance processes and ultimately improve quality and efficiency. The four most prevalent approaches are continuous quality improvement (CQI), Six Sigma, idealized design, and Lean management, each discussed below. Although all four approaches have some similarities with the National Learning Lab recommendations, Lean is the most highly correlated in that it focuses on eliminating waste, rework, and mistakes; these similarities are discussed later in this sidebar.

CQI

CQI is a management philosophy that involves improving or developing processes to meet or exceed customer expectations. The theories of Crosby, Juran, and most notably Deming, are rooted in CQI. Plan, do, check, act (PDCA) is often used in CQI. In the *plan* phase, problems with processes are identified using data to generate ideas and solutions. In the *do* phase, an agreed-upon intervention for correcting identified issues with the process is implemented. In the *check* phase, process changes are monitored for efficiency. In the *act* phase, the monitoring is reviewed and new issues or opportunities are identified. Then the PDCA cycle starts over to achieve continuous quality improvement.

Six Sigma

Six Sigma is a management philosophy of understanding the variation in a process and minimizing that variation, resulting in a Six Sigma level of performance (that is, 3.5 errors per 1,000,000 transactions). The Motorola Corporation is credited with initially developing Six Sigma as an internal quality initiative in the 1980s. The primary technique used in Six Sigma is DMAIC (define, measure, analyze, improve, and control). In the *define* stage, a process is identified and teams are formed. In the *measure* stage, data about the process and any variation within the process are collected. Then the data are *analyzed* for root causes to identify improvements. In the *improve* stage, the processes are implemented. Finally, in the *control* stage, the processes are monitored so that adherence to the new process is maintained.

Idealized Design

Idealized design is a methodology to help organizations transform processes, culture, and facilities. Within this methodology, an idealized process, facility, or culture is brainstormed. For example, a facility design might brainstorm around the concept of an ideal medication process, asking: What would the "safest" medication process look like without any economic, facility, or technological constraints? When the idealized process is developed, constraints and needs are identified. The organization might need technology and new software, certain facilities might need to change, and culture improvements to implement the idealized process will have to occur. Financial, cultural, and technological constraints also need to be identified. Then the ideal design must be compromised or changed to meet the identified constraints. It is also important to make sure that the design developed allows for innovation that can overcome the constraints.

(continued on page 27)

The Similarities of the National Learning Lab Recommendations and Quality Improvement Methodologies (continued)

Lean Thinking

Lean thinking is a principle-driven management philosophy aimed at identifying and eliminating waste. Toyota developed and uses this approach in all aspects of its operations. The Toyota Lean approach has 14 management principles and many tools to improve quality and efficiency. A Lean technique commonly cited is the Five Ss: Sort, simplify or straighten, sweep, standardize, and sustain. In the *sort* phase, items are reviewed to be kept or removed, then the items that are needed are organized so that people can identify them easily and simply. The area is cleaned and checked thoroughly in the *sweep* phase. In the *standardize* phase, everything in the process and area has its place, and everything is in its place. Finally, the new process is monitored to assure compliance so that the changes are *sustained.*

Most of the Lean principles are highly aligned with the National Learning Lab recommendations, particularly regarding the latent conditions. Table 1 below compares these methodologies.

Table 1: Comparison of Latent Conditions Addressed by National Learning Lab Recommendations and Lean Thinking Philosophy

Latent Conditions
- Noise reduction
- Scalability, adaptability, flexibility
- Visibility of patients to staff
- Patients involved with their care
- Standardization
- Automate where possible
- Minimize fatigue
- Immediate accessibility of information, close to the point of service
- Minimize transfers/hand-offs
- Minimize patient movement

Lean Principles
- Create continuous flow
- Don't batch
- Visual control
- Value stream
- Standardize work
- Pull versus push
- Proven technology
- Get quality right the first time
- Culture of stopping to fix problems

(continued on page 28)

The Similarities of the National Learning Lab Recommendations and Quality Improvement Methodologies (continued)

The Lean principles, discussed in more detail below, are highly correlated with the National Learning Lab recommendations. Safety is about creating processes that put caregivers in circumstances in which cognitive processes are influenced by the environment, process, and culture; in this way, mistakes are minimized, but when they do occur they do not harm patients. Hospitals should design conditions that people work in to support them doing the right things right. The National Learning Lab recommendations accomplish this objective, as do the Lean principles.

Create Continuous Flow, Don't Batch, Ensure Visual Control
When designing processes to be safe, it is best to work with one patient and one drug at a time, in an uninterrupted, focused way—that is, seeing one patient completely through the process. Doing this creates conditions in which the possibility of mixing up A with B is minimized, and completeness and accuracy are managed. For example, a nurse obtains one patient's medication, delivers the medication, and records the transaction before performing the same procedure on the next patient. In addition, completing this process in view of the patient will help with delivering complete, accurate care. "Out of sight, out of mind" fosters conditions of greater error. Thus, patient safety is maximized where there is continuous flow, no batching, and visual control.

Patient care in the intensive care unit (ICU) exemplifies these three concepts. In most ICUs, nurse-to-patient ratios are one to one, one to two, or one to three, and rooms have glass fronts so caregivers can view the patient from the nursing stations. This allows caregivers to have a much higher level of visual control, because they can always see the patient. Then each patient can be attended to as needed, then the next patient, and so on (continuous flow). The one-to-one/two/three ratio means little or no batching.

The perception is that patients have better outcomes in the ICU than on general medical-surgical floors where the staffing ratios are higher, and centralized nursing stations do not allow direct viewing of all the patients. Although it is not certain why this perception exists, there are some possible reasons, including the staffing ratios and the ability for quicker intervention with the patient. One-to-one-to-three ratios mean a caregiver is more focused on fewer patients, allowing for greater understanding of and attention to the patient's needs. In addition, if the patient's condition changes, the visibility of an ICU setting coupled with the low staffing ratio allows for a quick and timely intervention. In essence, the caregivers are a built-in rapid response team. Further, because ICU nurses perform services one at a time, completing the process while observing the patient throughout the process, conditions for cognitive failure and human error are minimized. In Lean definitions, the process exhibits continuous flow, lack of batching, and visual control.

Lean manufacturing experts also contend that this approach is more efficient. Visual control allows one to see the errors clearly; if they exist, they are allowed to affect the process only once because care is being delivered one step at a time, which does not affect other steps, as a batched process does. Lean experts also contend that this

(continued on page 29)

The Similarities of the National Learning Lab Recommendations and Quality Improvement Methodologies (continued)

approach is faster and therefore more efficient, although this may seem interventional.

Batching and then moving on to the next step in a process may seem more efficient. For example, in batching, an employee must repeat one step in a process and master it before the employee can move on to the next step in a process. It might seem that batching would be quicker and more efficient than continuous flow. However, the following example of a batching exercise can show how batching can actually be slower. Start with a stack of 6 to 10 papers and a group of 6 to 10 people. Have the first person sign all the papers and then pass the papers to the next person to sign, and so on until everyone has signed all the papers; have someone time this process. Then, change the process so that the first person signs and passes on the first piece of paper, signs and passes on the second piece of paper, and so on until each person has signed and passed on all the pages. Time this process as well. This process demonstrates doing work one step at a time in a continuous flow. The results will be faster for the continuous flow process than with the batching process.

Many instances of batching exist in hospitals (for example, in laboratory processes). The phlebotomist draws blood in the morning in a batch process—that is, he or she draws blood from multiple patients, after which the batched tubes of blood are sent to the lab. Usually multiple phlebotomists draw blood at the same time.

Another example occurs in colonoscopy suites. The first patients are scheduled consistent with the number of rooms (for example, five patients for five rooms). They all show up for the first appointment and flow through the process in a batch, and then are followed by another batched group of patients. One organization used a staggered schedule to change this process to a continuous flow of one patient at a time. This, coupled with other process changes, allowed the organization to double the number of patients with no increase in human or physical resources.[1]

Value Stream
Two of the National Learning Lab recommendations correlate with the value stream concept: minimizing hand offs and transfers. A study conducted by St. Joseph's Hospital, West Bend, Wisconsin, funded through an Agency for Healthcare Research and Quality grant, shows how prevalent transfers and hand offs are in hospitals. The study identified the hand offs and transfers in a process, and pointed out how often complete and accurate information is not provided during hand offs. As a result, hand offs and transfers should be discouraged because of the increased risk of error and the increased likelihood of harm to staff and patients. A process with no hand offs and no transfers would be the safest for patients and staff. If hand offs and transfers *do* occur, they must include complete and accurate information. But eliminating transfers and hand offs reinforces the concept of bringing services to the patient, and eliminating steps in a process or compressing processes is the Lean value stream.

(continued on page 30)

The Similarities of the National Learning Lab Recommendations and Quality Improvement Methodologies (continued)

Value stream and value mapping can be important tools to minimize hand offs and transfers. Assessing whether each step in a process brings value to the patient or caregivers can be a very effective way to compress or minimize hand offs or transfers. The following illustration shows how.

Historically, patients needing to be catheterized for an emergency heart blockage condition would often go through the following process: They would enter an emergency department (ED), register or be triaged in the waiting room or a triage space, be transferred to an ED room for diagnosis, be transferred to a preparation room or area for the catheterization, be transferred to the catheterization room for the procedure, be transferred to an ICU, be transferred to a step-down room, and finally be discharged. From the patient's point of view, the value received from the process is (1) being discharged after the procedure is performed; and (2) having a successful catheterization procedure. The remaining steps are not value-added to the patient; in addition, they can create transfers capable of creating conditions for error. The ideal situation for such a patient would be arriving at the hospital, going to the catheterization room for a successful procedure, and then being discharged. The process would be speedier and with an improved outcome. Many organizations that attempt to streamline catheterization processes have lowered the number of hand offs. Value mapping is an important tool to minimize hand offs and transfers.

Standardization

Standardizing routine work processes has many important effects that can improve the safety of patients and/or reduce error rates. The human brain creates patterns or schemata (as discussed in Chapter 1). When stimulated, these patterns work "subconsciously." Standardized processes allow these patterns to work accurately over and over again. Driving and operating a car would be an example. When someone learns to drive, he or she doesn't need to think consciously how to use the car key to turn the engine on or operate the windshield wipers or the radio. In fact, many people have had the experience of not actually remembering driving home, but getting there and doing so without an accident.

Thinking *consciously* can lead to fatigue and human error in routine functions. Nonstandardized processes require the use of short-term memory more than standardized processes do. The use of short-term memory is more error prone than "subconscious" schemata-driven behavior. Furthermore, when one is forced to use short-term memory in nonstandardized processes—thereby focusing on activities that could be done "subconsciously" if they were standardized—one cannot as easily focus on creative problem solving, such as assessment diagnosis, clinical intervention, and so on.

Toyota believes that standardization is the foundation for continuous improvement and employee empowerment—it could also be the foundation for employee morale and creativity. If a process is standardized through employee participation, then employees will

(continued on page 31)

The Similarities of the National Learning Lab Recommendations and Quality Improvement Methodologies (continued)

"own" the process and feel that their opinions are valued. The standardized process also creates a stable process that employees can evaluate for improvement. For example, one assumes that there are four ways to order medications: by phone, by fax, by mail, or by e-mail. These four methods bring complexity and lack of standardization, making it difficult to evaluate the efficacy of the ordering process. However, if one method, such as faxing, is chosen, then it is possible to evaluate its performance and improve as necessary. In addition, standardized processes allow employees to do their work "subconsciously," thereby freeing up energy and thought to brainstorm and come up with new ideas to improve processes. As a result, processes are continually improved, which improves employee morale.

Pull Versus Push Systems
Toyota believes that the most efficient and accurate way to organize a process is through a pull rather than a push system. When employees have completed their current assignment (continuous flow, one at a time, visible), they can start the next assignment (pulling). In a hospital, *pulling* would be starting with a new patient after the first patient is cared for, as opposed to an employee caring for patients all at once. It is easy to see how multitasking might increase, batching could occur, and stress could rise, all creating the conditions for more human error. Pull systems are safer.

Reliable Technology
"Automate where possible" is an important recommendation of the National Learning Lab. If one can replace a step or steps in a process with reliable technology, less error will occur. Reliable automated processes have less error than humans performing the same processes. There is one caution, however. Reliable, thoroughly tested technology that serves people and processes is also related to the unforeseen consequences of technology. Technology not implemented properly or not proven or tested could create more complexity and additional risks to patients and caregivers, creating different errors and adverse events. A reliable technology, though, can be an important tool to improve safety and quality for patients. It impacts fatigue, standardization, hand offs, complete and accurate information at the point of service, and enhanced communication.

Error Proofing
Once it becomes clear where human error occurs or could occur in a process, "error proofing" becomes important. In *The Psychology of Everyday Things*, Norman offers insight into how to error proof. The National Learning Lab recommendations identify latent conditions that pinpoint places where more errors will occur, and others where fewer errors will occur. For example, excess noise causes more error and therefore should be minimized, while standardization causes fewer errors and therefore should be maximized. Errors often happen when standardization is lacking, because complexity leads to error. Norman encourages the use of simplification, natural mapping, and affordance (when something does what someone naturally thinks it should do) to improve processes. Simplification and standardization are important for managing human error. Natural

(continued on page 32)

The Similarities of the National Learning Lab Recommendations and Quality Improvement Methodologies (continued)

mapping and affordance are concepts aimed at design consistent with what seems "natural."

The concept that Norman stresses the most, in connection with error proofing, is *forcing functions*. The principle here is not to allow the error to occur—it is much preferable to catch the error before it occurs (for example, computerized prescriber order entry systems that will not accept an order for the wrong dosage).

Another important concept in error proofing is recovery, which allows someone to change a decision before it results in harm or permanently creates risk. Software design provides many examples of the recovery function. The question, "Are you sure you want to (*delete? move?*)" and so on popping up on the computer screen illustrates the recovery concept.

Get Quality Right the First Time

In manufacturing, rework is very costly. When raw material proceeds through the process, the desire for speed and efficiency pushes employees to move the product along the production line. But if a deficiency exists when the product is inspected at the end, the product must be sent to another area to be corrected. The reality is that, overall, the production time increases when deficiencies exist, while efficiency takes less time. The alternative is to stop the manufacturing line and make sure the product is correctly developed at one station before it moves to the next station. Doing so is the most efficient and high-quality method. It also forces solving quality problems and creates awareness of design problems within processes, equipment, facilities, and technology at the source, or root cause. Rework is minimized and eliminated. Management needs to work with the employees performing the function to ensure that quality is in every step.

Hospitals are increasingly adopting the motto and philosophy of "stopping the line." In health care, though, "stopping the line" can be less apparent and seemingly more difficult, particularly in life-and-death situations. Imagine that a code team is rushing to a patient room and an important drug is missing on the crash cart. Caregivers do not stop to figure out at that moment why the drug is not present and how to prevent the problem from recurring before they attempt to save the patient. Time-outs are another example of stopping the line. Verifying a surgical patient, procedure, and supplies—"stopping the line" proactively—hopefully will catch any issue before surgery begins.

If a health care worker is involved with a clinical or support process and observes that someone is going to make a quality mistake or notices a process flaw, should he or she make an intervention to improve the circumstance? Are they, in fact, obligated to make the intervention? These are not always easy questions to answer. Obviously, the cultural impediments to create the best outcomes need to be resolved. These include retaliatory behaviors, blaming culture, just cultures, reporting culture, and learning cultures. The fact is, however, that without such interventions, the results could cause harm to patients.

Reference
1. Park Nicollet Health System, St. Louis Park, Minnesota.

Chapter 4
Applying the National Learning Lab Recommendations to the Safety Design Process

"Humans . . . behave clumsily . . . when the things they do are badly conceived, badly designed." (Donald Norman, *The Psychology of Everyday Things*. New York: Basic Books, 1988, p. vii.)

The traditional facility design process needs to be modified to focus on safety. This chapter will first outline the traditional facility design process and then show how it should be modified to focus on safety, using the National Learning Lab recommendations.

The Traditional Design Process

Outlining the traditional design process is the first step a hospital goes through so that the process can be compared with the new design process that focuses on patient safety as its guiding principle.

Table 4-1 illustrates the steps in the design process that hospitals traditionally take. The first step is to develop a Role and Program, which is a description of the hospital's projected volume, services, and financial constraints. Medical/surgical services, Labor, Delivery, Recovery, and Postpartum (LDRP) beds, intensive care unit (ICU), surgical services, and inpatient mental health would be examples. Forecasted volumes of proposed inpatient admissions at an assumed length of stay and an assumed average occupancy are translated into

> **Table 4-1. Steps in the Traditional Facility Design Process**
>
> Role and Program
> Functional Space Program
> Adjacencies (Block Diagrams)
> Schematic Design
> Design Development
> Construction Documents
> Construction

the proposed number of beds to be built. The proposed diagnostic services determine the size and types of diagnostic rooms. The number of surgical procedures forecast by type leads to the number of surgery and operating rooms needed. Employee and staffing patterns are also important components of the Role and Program. Although the major equipment and significant technologies proposed should also affect the Role and Program, detailed equipment planning and technology planning typically does not occur at this stage.

When complete, the Role and Program is translated into a Functional Space Program, which is a room-by-room description of the proposed facility project—for example, five surgical suites at 400 square feet per room. This adds up to the "functional space" necessary, to which is typically added a circulation factor—a net-to-gross square footage factor that allows for hallways and other connecting spaces, storage space (often underestimated), and other utility and support spaces—to arrive at the gross square footage of the project. If a cost per square foot assumption is made, multiplying the cost per square foot by the number of gross square feet yields a construction cost figure—an important base of the facility's development budget.

The next step, block diagrams, or adjacencies, is where related departments and services are placed next to each other or in vertical relation to each other. It is during this step in traditional design that the site, philosophies of relationships between patients and materials, and departments whose relationships are functionally related are considered. This step also considers the "traffic patterns" (flow) of patients, staff, and materials with particular attention to maintaining separation of public/private and clean/dirty zones.

The next stage is schematic design, which is a schematic drawing of blocks of adjacencies within departments (for example, radiology rooms).

Detailed design and drawings for every room occur during the design development stage. The location of outlets, lights, and fixed equipment locations are determined; detailed equipment and technology plans are created during this stage.

Finally, in the last two stages, the design development drawings are translated into construction documents and then the building is built using the construction documents.

In a traditional design process, patient safety is typically not addressed during any of these stages, nor is the impact of the facility's technology and equipment on patient safety explored. In addition, patient safety design principles, latent conditions, and active failures and their impact on the traditional facility design process are not considered. Existing staffing patterns and processes are assumed to continue in the traditional design process, thus mitigating the importance that facilities, with their technology and equipment focused on safety, can have on staffing patterns and processes. Human factors analysis focused on safety will have a significant impact on facilities, equipment, technology, and processes of a hospital.

Safety Design Process Recommendations

Participants of the National Learning Lab were instrumental in developing a set of safety-driven design principles that would guide the design process. The National Learning Lab outlined eight steps that can be used to reach the goal of safety in design (*see* Table 4-2, right). These design principles are aimed at minimizing latent conditions and reducing active failures, thus creating a facility design process focused on patient safety. This chapter discusses each step to illustrate how to implement each recommendation into a design process, as well as how to apply the safety design principles to minimize latent conditions and active failures and enhance patient safety within a hospital.

Table 4-2. Safety Design Process Recommendations

1. Matrix development
2. FMEA at each stage of design
3. Patients/families involved in design process
4. Equipment planning from Day 1
5. Mock-ups from Day 1
6. Design for the vulnerable patient
7. Articulation of a set of principles for measurement
8. Establishment of a checklist for current/future design

Matrix Development

The matrix development process involves brainstorming ideas and design features National Learning Lab's safety design principles. It is also used to prioritize the po tures, technology, and equipment to maximize safety while maintaining the hosp~~____ _____ ____~~ available capital. Evidence-based design is an important concept to keep in mind during the brainstorming process. Simply stated, evidence-based design refers to design decisions that are based on the most current information and research available, much as evidence-based medicine is based on scientific research. The Center for Health Design (http://www.healthdesign.org) provides information on evidence-based design and the latest research in this area. It is worth noting that one of the center's programs is called *Pebble Projects*—a designation for hospitals that have focused on safety by design—and St. Joseph's Hospital in West Bend, Wisconsin, which was the key sponsor and organizer of the National Learning Lab, is one of the Pebble Projects.[1]

Using the quality functional deployment technique, it places the voice of the customer on one axis and the technical requirement is placed on the other axis. For example, in the automobile industry (one of the early adopters of this technique), customers might prefer that car doors not make a loud noise when closing; to technically accomplish this goal, a list of requirements follows. (The "voice of the customers" is the National Learning Lab requirement for active failures reduction and latent conditions management. Other "voices" are the design principles discussed in Chapter 3 on preparing for facility-safe design and capital cost requirements. *See* Table 4-3 on page 36.)

The y (vertical) axis of the matrix lists the results of the National Learning Lab, other design principles, key customer groups, employees, physicians, nurses, and patients. Patients could be subdivided into services such as inpatient, outpatient, emergency, and surgical; gender; and conditions such as heart, orthopedic, and so on. The x (horizontal) axis has the same items as the y axis, as well as process changes needed, facility square footage, timing, capital, operating cost, and responsible party, as shown in Table 4-3 on page 36.

Participants can then brainstorm a master list of design features based on the vertical axis. For example, visibility of patients to staff, a safety design principle, might include lighting source, level of natural lighting, windows in doors, and cameras for every patient care area.

The design team (architects, mechanical/electrical/plumbing architects, the equipment planner, the owner's representative, and the general contractor) and administrative personnel, physicians, and other clinical representatives should all be involved in developing the matrix. In addition, the results of the technology fair, market research information, focus group information, surveys, and other information (discussed in Chapter 3) should be incorporated into the matrix development process.

After brainstorming, the team should schedule additional time to complete the y axis. All the design, technology, or equipment ideas to meet the design principles need to be compared to each other, for example, does the "visibility of patients to staff" principle affect other design principles? Design principles are not prioritized at this point, but participants can judge how they could incorporate design features that would affect multiple safety design principles.

Usually the matrix process will create ideas that materially exceed the capital budget. Comparing the safety effect of a design feature against the capital and operating costs is one way to help prioritize which features to implement and when (*see* Table 4-4, below).

Another strategy is to determine which ideas need to be implemented as part of the facility development, and which ideas can be delayed until after the opening of the new facility. For example, wiring for a certain technology needs to be done as part of the construction, but the acquisition of that tech-

Table 4-3. Matrix Form

	Visibility of Patients	Standardization	Precarious Events	Employee Safety	Physician Safety	Patients	Inpatient	Outpatient	Emergency	Surgical	Efficient	Healing Environment	Process Changes	Facility Sq Footage	Timing	Capital	Operating Costs	Person Responsible
Visibility of Patients																		
Standardization																		
Precarious Events																		
Employee Safety																		
Physician Safety																		
Patients																		
Inpatient																		
Outpatient																		
Emergency																		
Surgical																		
Efficient																		
Healing Environment																		

Table 4-4. Design Features: Cost Versus Safety

Operating and Capital Costs	Enter Design Feature	Impact on Safety		
		Low	Medium	High
	Low			
	Medium			
	High			

nology may be delayed until after the completion of the construction. The matrix development process can be an exciting, creative, and useful way to capitalize on an organization's investment in a new facility that maximizes safety.

Other process recommendations of the National Learning Lab need to be implemented to effectively complete the matrix process. Equipment Planning from Day 1, Mock-ups from Day 1, Articulation of a Set of Principles for Measurement, Establishment of a Checklist for Current/Future Designs, Patients/Families Involved in the Design Process, Design for the Vulnerable Patient, and failure mode and effects analysis all contribute to the matrix development and the completion of the Role and Program, Functional Space Program, and Adjacencies (Block Diagrams) stages of the facility design process. When the matrix is complete, the schematic and design development phases can begin.

Failure Mode and Effects Analysis (FMEA)

Failure mode and effects analysis (FMEA) is a proactive tool used in manufacturing for years that has recently begun to be used in health care. The Joint Commission requires organizations to conduct one proactive risk assessment, such as FMEA, each year.[2]

FMEA proactively assesses potential failures in a process (pFMEA), the effect of the potential failure, and what changes could prevent, control, or protect against the failure. In health care, the processes, not the designs, are typically evaluated. For example, a physician on rounds could order a patient's medication either by communicating with a nurse at the bedside or the central nursing station or by writing an order on the patient's chart. Later, the clerical staff on the floor would review the medication order with a nurse, type the order, and communicate with the pharmacy. Failures in this process could include misrepresentation of a verbal order, transcription errors, a nurse missing an error in the order, the wrong patient being connected to the medication order, an incorrect medication being ordered for the patient's condition, or an error in the medication dosage, route, or time.

The effect of the failure is judged around three dimensions: severity, frequency of occurrence, and detectability. One judges how often the errors were likely to happen (occurrence), how serious the consequences of the error would be (severity), and how likely the error would be discovered before or after the injury (detection). The severity, occurrence, and detection are typically scored on a scale from 1 to 10. The severity, occurrence, and detection scores are multiplied and the resulting number is used to rank order or prioritize the potential failure to be corrected. Solutions are then brainstormed around the failures and, after agreeing on the best solution, they are implemented. In the example given above, computerized prescriber order entry (CPOE) with decision support could correct most of the possible failures identified in the pharmacy process.

Process FMEA

A pFMEA is "an engineering technique used to define, identify, prioritize, and eliminate known or potential failures, problems, errors from the system, design, process, or services before they reach the customer."[3] This tool is aimed at preventing accidents, but it does not require a prior accident or a close call to use. The recommended steps in a pFMEA are as follows:

1. Develop a team of employees to flowchart the process.
2. Identify possible failures (the failure modes) for each step in the process and each link (hand off) between steps.
3. For each failure mode, identify its potential effects.
4. Determine the severity of the effects.
5. Determine the frequency of occurrence of the failures.
6. Determine the detectability of the failures.
7. Prioritize the failure modes, such as by calculating the Risk Priority Number (RPN) (severity × frequency × detectability). Each of these three dimensions is rated on a scale from 1 to 10, making 1,000 the largest possible score for a single failure mode. The purpose of the RPN is to prioritize the failures to target first. High severity scores should also be targeted.
8. For the highest priority failure modes, identify the causes of each failure.
9. Based on the identified causes, develop an action plan for redesigning the process to minimize risk.

A sample FMEA worksheet is illustrated in Figure 4-1 on page 39.

The application of pFMEAs is important, but fulfilling the National Learning Lab's recommendation to conduct an FMEA at each design phase also requires the understanding and application of design FMEAs.

Design FMEA

A design FMEA (dFMEA) is the application of an FMEA to facility design, with its equipment and technology.[4]* A dFMEA assumes the process performs accurately and the failure mode being brainstormed relates potential failure in design (adjacencies, for example), to meet the design intent. Severity in dFMEAs represents the seriousness of the failure of the facility design as it relates to the processes and to its customers. Potential causes of the failure need to be identified to indicate design weakness that could result in the failure. RPN is calculated as it is in pFMEAs, with high RPN and high severity receiving the highest priority.

The FMEA process is time intensive and numerically based, even though the judgments of severity, occurrence, and detection are subjective and based on experience. dFMEAs should be applied during the Adjacencies (Block Diagrams), Schematic Design, and Design Development stages.

Adjacencies or Block Diagram FMEAs

The first application is performing a dFMEA on the Adjacencies (Block Diagrams). First, the architects work with initial input from department heads, meet with the leadership team and others, and create a set of adjacencies. The adjacencies are then placed on the site, based on philosophies about the relationship of supplies movement to patient movement, which functions should be near others, and how many entrances there need to be and what their functions are; all this must be balanced with the architects' design vision of the building's appearance. For example, placing a hospital's ICU on the floor above the emergency department (ED) allows for failures during typical processes such as staff having to leave the ICU and going to the ED to pick up patients; that is, the ICU is left shortstaffed, and there

---

* Ron Atkinson from General Motors provided much helpful assistance and information on dFMEAs

Failure Mode and Effects Analysis (FMEA) Worksheet

Process/Product_____
Team Leader _____

Core Team_____ Key Date _____

FMEA Number ____
FMEA Date (original) ____
FMEA Date (revision) ____

Column 1	Column 2	Column 3	C4	Column 5	C6	Column 7	C8	C9	Column 10	Column 11	Action Results				
Item/ Function	Potential Failure Mode(s)	Potential Effect(s) of Failure	SEVERITY	Potential Causes/ Mechanism(s) of Failure	OCCURRENCE	Current Process/ Design Controls	DETECTION	RPN	Recommended Action (s)	Responsibility & Target Completion Date	Actions Taken	New Severity	New Occurrence	New Detection	Revised RPN

Process/Product <u>Appt Scheduling</u>
Team Leader <u>Diana Scott</u>

Failure Mode and Effects Analysis (FMEA) Worksheet

Core Team <u>G. Porto, D. Scott, J. Doe, R. Smith, B. Jones, M. Lane</u> Key Date <u>1/30/02</u>

FMEA Number <u>2002-01</u>
FMEA Date (original) <u>1/15/02</u>
FMEA Date (revision) <u>3/01/02</u>

Column 1	Column 2	Column 3	C4	Column 5	C6	Column 7	C8	C9	Column 10	Column 11	Action Results				
Item/ Function	Potential Failure Mode(s)	Potential Effect(s) of Failure	SEVERITY	Potential Causes/ Mechanism(s) of Failure	OCCURRENCE	Current Process/ Design Controls	DETECTION	RPN	Recommended Action (s)	Responsibility & Target Completion Date	Actions Taken	New Severity	New Occurrence	New Detection	Revised RPN
Physician communicates date of follow-up appt. to receptionist	Writing illegible	Pt gets wrong appt: ▪Dissatisfaction ▪Changes MDs ▪Injury ▪Death	10	Reliance on written communication	10	Receptionist double checks w/physician when can't read writing.	7	700	Implement checklist format for recording date of follow-up appointment.	Jane Doe, R.N.	Checklist developed by Jane Doe's team Checklist piloted during the month of Feb. Changes implemented and pilot repeated. Changes adopted unit-wide April 2002.	10	2	1	20
	Physician forgets to write date	Pt gets no appt: ▪Dissatisfaction ▪Changes MDs ▪Injury ▪Death	10	Dependence on vigilance Dependence on memory	10	Receptionist double checks form. Retrospective chart reviews (sampling).	6 / 9	600 / 900	Implement automated reminder.	Rob Smith	Reminder designed and tested 2/01 Reminder piloted 3/02 Software conflicts identified, revisions to programming 4/02 Repeat pilot done 4/02 Training of staff completed 5/02. Change implemented 5/0	10	1	4	40
	Physician writes wrong date	Pt gets wrong appt: ▪Dissatisfaction ▪Changes MDs ▪Injury ▪Death	10	Mental lapse due to fatigue, interruption or distraction Judgment error	5 / 2	Receptionist double checks. Retrospective chart reviews (sampling).	9 / 9	450 / 180	Implement standardized protocol for follow-up appointment. 100% chart audit within 1 week	Beth Jones, M.D.	Review of literature, survey of practitioners done 2/01 Draft protocol developed 3/02 Draft protocol presented to Dept. PI Committee 4/02 Revisions to protocol 6/02 Medical, unit staff educated 6/02 Protocol Implemented 7/02 Further revisions to protocol 9/92	10 / 10	3 / 1	2 / 2	60 / 20

Figure 4-1. Sample FMEA Worksheet.
This figure includes a sample FMEA worksheet that can be used during the pFMEA process.

is the risk of elevator difficulties. Therefore, the recommendation in this case could be to place the ICU *next to* the ED, thus avoiding such risks.

The dFMEA assesses or investigates how the adjacencies cause failures; it evaluates adjacencies against key processes that cause failure. Performing a dFMEA assumes the processes function as designed. If a process flows through the adjacencies as specified, how do the adjacencies cause failures? To answer this, the design team should focus on key processes related to vulnerable patients, choosing processes in which moving a patient could create a vulnerable condition, or when the patients' admitting conditions could make them vulnerable. Examples of such processes are transferring a patient from the ED to the ICU, from the ED to surgery, from the ICU to radiology, and from the ED to radiology.

It is useful to apply a dFMEA analysis to routine, common processes to determine whether the adjacencies harm that process (for example, patients arriving at the ED for treatment, then needing a lab test, and whether these two departments are in close proximity; or material flows such as delivering supplies, and whether food and supplies are delivered through the same corridors as the movement of patients and staff, which could lead to interruptions and delays). A dFMEA assessment is also useful for high-volume processes such as adjacencies of the ED to radiology, where many patients coming through the ED have to go for a radiology exam before being brought back to the ED. If the two departments are on different floors, if elevator use is needed, or if the horizontal adjacencies are too large, then the risks multiply.

The dFMEA should also test the flow of materials to a patient (registration, supplies, laundry, lab draws, pharmacy, food) and away from a patient (blood tissue for examination), waste (infected or clean), laundry, and environmental concerns (can/glass/paper/plastic/food). Analyzing this flow assesses the objective of separating public activities from private activities; or in other words, onstage versus offstage. Separation can allow staff to better focus on their activities and not encumber patients and visitors with observing private activities, with the overall effect of improving the care experience and minimizing distractions that could cause error.

Teams can be formed to perform the dFMEAs, with each team being assigned a process to assess. The traditional dFMEA format for prioritizing failure modes is to rate severity from 1 to 10, occurrence from 1 to 10, and detection from 1 to 10, but this may be too complex and time consuming. A simplified sample form that could be used for the exercise is included in Figure 4-2 (page 41). Key concepts used in this new form include judging the adjacencies failure against the safety design principles. Other design principles such as efficiency and health environments are also assessed. Again, the assumption is that processes are performing perfectly as specified. Another key concept shown in the new form is scoring: severity and occurrence are scored simply as low, medium, and high. This is a more time-efficient method of assessing a potential adjacency failure.

The outcome of the exercise is to determine if any of the adjacencies should be changed. Therefore, the teams should determine how the adjacency failure (that is, any failure of a process that is the result of the adjacencies) could be eliminated or minimized through an adjacency change. Failures should be assessed for their severity and occurrence. Adjacency failures with a high severity and a low, medium, or high occurrence should be evaluated; the adjacencies then should be changed to eliminate the failures. Varying views exist on whether medium severity/occurrence and low severity/occurrence failures need to be assessed for adjacency changes. Many participants of dFMEA focused on safety feel that only medium severity with high or medium occurrence should be evaluated.

Although the organization and architects consider much when recommending adjacencies, material changes in adjacencies could occur as a result of the dFMEAs. Using dFMEAs during the adjacency stage should assess the effect the adjacencies have on safety design principles. Do the adjacencies cause

---

APPENDIX 11   FAILURE MODE AND EFFECTS ANALYSIS WORKSHEET

St. Joseph's Community Hospital of West Bend
a member of SynergyHealth

> Failure Mode and Effects Analysis
> (FMEA Worksheet)

Process: _____

Team Leader: _____
Core Team: _____

Potential Failure/ Effect Mode(s) (day/night)	Severity/Occurrence			Adjacency Changes to Minimize or Eliminate Potential Failure/Effect	Recommended Adjacency Change	Other Action Results	
	High	Med	Low				
						Process Issues or Changes	Design Features within Depart.

Figure 4-2. Sample Worksheet for Rating Severity.
This is a sample worksheet that St. Joseph's Hospital used to determine the severity and occurrence.

Source: St. Joseph's Hospital, West Bend, WI. Used with permission.

"failures" in meeting the design principles? Fatigue, noise, and flexibility are affected by adjacencies. Active failures such as medication errors and patient falls could be affected by adjacencies. Hand offs/transfers could be increased or minimized by the adjacencies.

Schematic FMEA

dFMEAs should also be applied to schematics, when key processes within departments and within rooms are developed. Each department identifies the key processes that occur in key rooms to determine room adjacencies. An example could be patient room design. Teams are assigned to assess the failures and effects of meeting safety design principles in the patient room. They should assess vulnerable patients (such as a patient having surgery) and patients in vulnerable places (such as patients being moved/handed off between treatment areas). Using the dFMEA provides a deeper understanding of designing complex rooms where patients, technology, equipment, and staff interface. Many configurations of patient rooms could be tested: back-to-back or truly standardized, single alcoves or double alcoves, one or two entrances, having the bathroom at the head of the bed or across from the patient, having showers separate from the rest of the bathroom, or having a centralized shower. The dFMEAs should be coupled with ideas from focus groups of past or prospective patients and their families.

Design Development FMEA

Implementing dFMEAs in the Design Development stage results in a greater focus on failures and the effects caused by a room and its components, such as hardware, headwalls, lighting fixtures, and equipment; on patients and staff performing normal processes within the room; or on vulnerable conditions within the room. This process could be called a room-by-room dFMEA. Again, the purpose is to assess the failures against the safety design principles.

Figure 4-3 (pages 43–44) includes an example of a new form that can be used to describe the key processes in the room and vulnerable processes (those that are vulnerable to failure), failures caused by not meeting functional requirements, solution descriptions about whether the failure is a design failure or a process change, the guiding principles failure, the current score (frequency, severity, and scope of impact), and the proposed solution score (frequency, severity, and scope of impact). *Scope of impact* means the breadth of the failure: Does it relate only to that room or does it have departmental- or facilitywide impact? An example could be a failure identified in the gastrointestinal procedure room, such as cords on the floor. Some of the effects of this failure could be lack of standardization, staff injury, and equipment damage; booms can be added as the proposed solution. Similarly, lack of easy access to portable oxygen tanks on the rehabilitation unit can be a design failure, particularly for vulnerable patients—therefore, a centralized space could be designed to solve the problem.

FMEA Summary

Although traditional FMEAs can be laborious and time-consuming, they can be modified to be valuable tools in designing a facility focused on patient safety. Adjacencies, departmental adjacencies, and detailed room drawings can be significantly changed as a result of the exercise. The team members assessing the different dFMEAs may bring bias with them, of course; this should be expected. What one person considers high severity, another might consider low severity, or a potential failure to one person might not be a potential failure to another. But there is a positive to this diversity of opinions: Staff can learn from each other about risks that exist within the hospital that could lead to harm.

ST. JOSEPH'S COMMUNITY HOSPITAL OF WEST BEND, INC. - NEW LIFE CENTER

Facility Standards	Cognitive Block Diagram *Common Understanding of Process*	Failures Associated with Block Diagram *Not meeting functional requirements*	Solution Descriptions	Solutions *Design Failure or Process Change? Simple Solution, Yes or No?*	Guiding Principle *Failure If Yes, which one?*	Current *1=low; 10=high* Frequency	Severity	Scope of Impact	Score	Proposed Solution *(if applicable) 1=low; 10=high* Frequency	Severity	Scope of Impact	Score
Fire Alarm *Code Carts* *Fire Extinguishers* *Phones (standard locations, not for routine staff use)* *Pyxis/Medication/Rooms (Clean/Dirty Linen Carts)* *C-section vs. OR Layout* *Med Gases* *Signage (wording, location, etc.)*													
Patient Confidentiality (HIPAA)		Nurse's station conversation flows into wait room (Current nurse's station conversation flows into patient room LDRP-4)	Expand waiting area by adding partial walls with 1/2 walls with aquarium (fire screens)	Design	Noise, Healing Environment	8	9	6	432	2	9	6	108
		Future elevator location decreased waiting room space							0				0
			Additional waiting room space at end of patient hall causes increased visitor traffic flow past patient rooms - 24 hours/day - increased conversation by visitors passing by pt rooms at night hours	Design									

ST. JOSEPH'S COMMUNITY HOSPITAL OF WEST BEND, INC. - Surgical Services (Endo/Procedural Room)

24 Hour Processes *Major Processes*	Cognitive Block Diagram *Common Understanding of Process*	Failures Associated with Block Diagram *Not meeting functional requirements*	Solution Descriptions	Solutions *Design Failure or Process Change? Simple Solution, Yes or No?*	Guiding Principle *Failure If Yes, which one?*	Current *1=low; 10=high* Frequency	Severity	Scope of Impact	Score	Proposed Solution *(if applicable) 1=low; 10=high* Frequency	Severity	Scope of Impact	Score
Drop down gases vs. wall mounted Booms in GI/procedure rooms (small vs. 2 retractable columns) min 2 suctions									0				0
		Cords on floor	Tour other GIs to inquire into booms for procedure room from various vendors May cause change in design		Safety Standardization Working in the dark Potential false optic damage with cords on the floor					0	8	8	8	512

ST. JOSEPH'S COMMUNITY HOSPITAL OF WEST BEND, INC. - Surgical Services (PACU)

24 Hour Processes *Major Processes*	Cognitive Block Diagram *Common Understanding of Process*	Failures Associated with Block Diagram *Not meeting functional requirements*	Solution Descriptions	Solutions *Design Failure or Process Change? Simple Solution, Yes or No?*	Guiding Principle *Failure If Yes, which one?*	Current *1=low; 10=high* Frequency	Severity	Scope of Impact	Score	Proposed Solution *(if applicable) 1=low; 10=high* Frequency	Severity	Scope of Impact	Score
Visibility of Patient's Monitors			A. Wireless communication for order entry for first floor pt care areas (ie: beside order entry)		Standardization				0	5	5	5	125
			B. Standardize monitors housewide (especially for C. Wire for cameras						0	8	10	9	720
Transportation * Patient in room * Patient in elevator * Patient to dept. * Patient to recovery		D. Elevator breakdown (access to back-up elevator thru public area)	D. No pt elevators in current facility so 10 for all areas						0	0	0	0	0
									0	4	4	4	64
		E. Crossing of Inpt and Outpt in hallway	E. Refer to "D"						0	6	6	6	216
		Question raised about PACU pts - visibility							0				0

(continued on page 44)

Figure 4-3. Sample Form for Describing Key Processes.

This sample form can be used to describe the key processes in the room and vulnerable processes, the failures caused by not meeting functional requirements, solution descriptions about whether the failure is a design failure or a process change, the guiding principles failure, the current score (frequency, severity, and scope of impact), and the proposed solution score (frequency, severity, and scope of impact).

Source: St. Joseph's Hospital, West Bend, WI. Used with permission.

ST. JOSEPH'S COMMUNITY HOSPITAL OF WEST BEND, INC. -ICU & RT

24 Hour Processes (Major Processes)	Cognitive Block Diagram (Common Understanding of Process)	Failures Associated with Block Diagram (Not meeting functional requirements)	Solution Descriptions	Solutions (Design Failure or Process Change? Simple Solution, Yes or No?)	Guiding Principle (Failure If Yes, which one?)	Current (1=low, 10=high)				Proposed Solution (if applicable) (1=low; 10=high)			
						Frequency	Severity	Scope of Impact	Score	Frequency	Severity	Scope of Impact	Score
1. Admission	Direct (ambu or walk-in) ED Inpt. Trfr OR admits	East Wing - 3rd floor - taking patient around nursing station - must horseshoe bed around nursing station to elevator	Redesign or pass thru nursing station	Design	Vuln Pt, Minimize Fatigue, Precarious Events	3	6	5	90	3	6	1	18
		Transporter for walk-in pts.		Process issue									
ICU Room	Patient room doors	Door opening (breakaway vs. larger opening door)	Larger opening, wider slider	Design	Fatigue, Safety, Vuln. Pt, Visibility	8	8	5	320	8	2	1	16
		Obstruction hallway...room Large portion of room unusable (critical area of the room)							0				0
		Visibility of nurse to pt with wall							0				0
Med room	OK												
Team Report		Checking locker space (garden level vs. ICU coat/purse lockers							0				0
PF Room		Location - access to pt.											
Miscellaneous Issues		Central scheduler for direct admits? Or call ICU direct							0				0
		Back-up for transporters if busy							0				0
		Designate elevators use - standardize (Elevator 5 for M/S to ICU)											
		RT Supply storage based on process											
		Medical records based on process											
		PFT based on process											
		ICU Supply Storage based on process											
		Security (in hospital & parking lots) Cameras Staff Back-up plan Crisis team											

Figure 4-3. Sample Form for Describing Key Processes. (continued)

Another complexity of this process is the amount of design principles that need to be met. Some solutions solve a failure in one design principle while creating a failure in another design principle. For example, it might be possible to observe six ICU rooms from a centralized nursing station. In a truly standardized ICU, at some point a nurse at the nursing station could view patients' feet but not their heads. If the ICU staff feels that the design principle of visibility of patients to staff is more important than standardization of the ICU layout, then the design can change to reflect this. One part of the solution could be to use glass partitions in the ICU, which would allow nurses to observe patients and anticipate their condition changes by actually seeing the changes in their condition (for example, head movement). This can also add to patient safety in that observing the patient's head helps the staff relate the correct patient to the documentation for that patient. One proposed solution to the ICU situation in this example could be to change the fully standardized ICU room to a half-standardized room on one side of the nursing station and a half-standardized room on the other side of the nursing station.

As the team conducts the dFMEA exercises, they might notice that the focus on safety creates an efficient facility and promotes a healing environment. Standardization, minimized fatigue, and complete and accurate information are design features that can increase efficiency. Eliminating noise, lighting choices, and involving patients in their care are design features that can create a healing environment.

Patients/Families Involved in Design Process

Information from patient surveys, market research information, general focus groups, focus groups for clinical rooms, and including patients on design teams are good ways to involve patients and families in the design process. As a result, general design issues such as entrances and adjacencies can be determined by the "voice of the customer." For example, consider asking patients whether the hospital should have multiple entrances for patients and families or one common entrance, what existing services need improvement, and which design features should be added to improve them. Focus groups can also discuss what new services to add to a particular area. Although one concern of using focus groups is the amount of time and expense involved without any new insights being revealed, experience has shown that although employees are very knowledgeable and have many years of accumulated experience, the insight from patients offers invaluable assistance.

Equipment Planning from Day 1

Most traditional design processes perform equipment planning during the Schematic Design and/or Design Development stages. Detailed room-by-room equipment lists are prepared. Equipment that can be moved or continued to be used is ascertained, and then the remaining needs are listed, leading to the final list of necessary equipment. However, the impact of equipment on human error and safety is usually not explored. Hospitals typically use multiple vendors with different models of one piece of equipment, thus causing complexity that in turn could lead to employees committing more errors. For example, if medication pumps from different vendors are available for use, and the different models have different rules for usage, the resulting confusion could cause an employee to misprogram a pump, thus harming a patient.

The National Learning Lab recommends that an equipment and technology consultant (if one is employed by the hospital) and a full-time internal equipment planner be involved in the new design process, starting from day one. The new internal equipment planner position, along with the consultant, if used, allows proper input into the matrix process, helping to maximize safety within the available capital budget and ensuring proper equipment and technology planning throughout the design stages.

Mock-ups from Day 1

Mock-up designs for many patient rooms, including the ICU, the medical/surgical unit, the LDR or LDRP, medication rooms, storage areas, and surgical rooms, should begin immediately. Many different types of mock-ups exist, from tape on the floor to two- or three-dimensional computer-generated models to physical construction. Mock-ups of specific room or service elements—for example, the supply cupboards for a pharmacy work area—should also occur. Physicians, nurses, staff, patients, and family members should be invited to view and evaluate the rooms. Suggestion forms placed in each room can encourage feedback.

The mock-up rooms can serve two functions in addition to designing a safer environment: simulations of systems and future education and orientation. Simulations on redesigned or current processes, such as routine functions, medication delivery in a patient room, or complex circumstances such as an emergency heart failure response code, can occur in mock-up rooms. Training that occurs until the remodeled or new space is completed can help minimize transition errors that might occur while moving into the new facility.

Design for the Vulnerable Patient

Patients can be vulnerable because of their admitting condition, such as open-heart surgery patients, a 90-year-old frail elderly patient with serious pneumonia, or a pediatric patient. Patients can also become vulnerable from routine care processes or from facility design. For example, a healthy 26-year-old having surgery to remove an ovarian cyst is vulnerable during care processes such as anesthesia and postsurgery, and when transfers or hand offs occur (which facility design affects). Patients in facilities designed to accommodate these vulnerabilities will experience a safer care experience.

Safer facilities will exist for all patients when vulnerabilities for serious conditions or care processes have been minimized. For example, rooms properly designed for a code (that is, an emergency heart failure response) should have features such as a door that is large enough for emergency carts to pass through easily, space on both sides of the patient and the foot of the bed to provide emergency care, outlets and medical gases that are easily accessible, and proper lighting. A ventilated patient must be in a room with large door openings that allow for easy access to equipment and the proper space to house the ventilator, as well as enough room to allow the caregivers to provide care. If the space around the beds, door widths, and outlet locations are sized for these conditions, they are probably sized for all conditions. When a patient is transferred from the ICU and needs an ICU nurse to accompany him or her, the other ICU patients can become vulnerable because there are suddenly fewer staff available. Proper design can help minimize or eliminate these vulnerabilities.

Articulation of a Set of Principles for Measurement

Potential sources for the principles of measurement are the general design principles discussed in Chapter 3, and the results of the National Learning Lab: Latent Conditions (*see* Table 2-3, page 18), Active Failures (*see* Table 2-4, page 18), and Safety Culture Recommendations (*see* Table 2-5, page 19). All of these principles can be measured either qualitatively or quantitatively. For example, minimizing fatigue can be measured by a fatigue scale survey such as the Piper Fatigue Survey (http://www.propax.com/survey/citation.shtml). The level of standardization can also be surveyed. Medication errors can be measured along with other active failures. Safety culture can be measured by using a Likert scale survey or by participating with national safety culture instruments such as the Agency for Healthcare Research and Quality's Patient Safety Climate Survey. The ability of the organization to be patient centered could be measured by a patient satisfaction survey.

Establishment of a Checklist for Current/Future Design

As the aviation industry has learned, it is easy to be distracted through interruptions or boredom, causing a lack of routine engine checks and possibly leading to a crash. The aviation industry now requires checklists for routine preflight preparation. In health care, establishing a checklist for safety by design—and having all participants complete it—has multiple outcomes. Primarily, it has the effect of ensuring that everyone has thought about the design principles. This process can change culture, developing staff awareness of the safety design principles and their impact on safety. It also allows organizations to see the application across departments and services, which helps with coordination and learning across departments. Finally, using a checklist has the effect of helping a person or a department remember to explore design principles.

Table 4-5. Latent Conditions

1. Noise reduction
2. Scalability, adaptability, flexibility
3. Visibility of patients to staff
4. Patients involved with their care
5. Standardization
6. Automation where possible
7. Minimizing fatigue
8. Immediate accessibility of information, close to the point of service
9. Minimizing patient transfers/ hand offs

When a hospital or health care organization begins the process of applying the National Learning Lab recommendations to its facility design process, with a focus on safety in design, it will begin to benefit from significant changes that can maximize the potential for patient safety and help create a healing environment for patients and staff.

The Significance of Latent Conditions and Their Impact on Safety Design

When designing a new health care facility or remodeling an existing facility, it is important to identify and prevent active errors and latent conditions. As explained previously, *latent conditions* are organizational issues that create conditions for error; these conditions may lie dormant and unnoticed within the system until they combine with other conditions to cause harm. Table 4-5 at left lists the latent conditions identified during the National Learning Lab as areas of concern to patient safety. These areas should be addressed during the facility design process focused on safety.

Noise Reduction

A report by the World Health Organization indicates that noise interferes with communication, creates distractions, affects cognitive performance and concentration, causes annoyance, and contributes to stress and fatigue.[5] Mental activities involving a demand on working memory are particularly sensitive to noise and can result in performance degradation. In one study, anesthesia residents exhibited reduced mental efficiency and poorer short-term memory under the noisy conditions of an operating room averaging 77 decibels.[6] (For comparison, a motorcycle is approximately 95 decibels while a quiet library is approximately 45–50 decibels.)

In addition to safety considerations, noise affects the quality of the healing environment for patients. It can elevate blood pressure, increase pain, alter quality of sleep, and reduce overall perceived patient satisfaction. Studies in pediatric ICUs have shown that noise routinely disrupts sleep that is necessary for patient comfort or recovery.[7]

The nature of sound, specifically its reverberation rate—how long the sound remains—has a direct effect on the noise level. A long reverberation rate leads to greater opportunity for sounds to blend together, thus increasing the noise level. With speech communication, a longer reverberation time combined with background noise makes speech perception increasingly difficult.

Many design features can minimize noise. Examples include no overhead paging; quiet floor coverings (such as carpet or rubber); "quiet" heating, ventilation, and air-conditioning (HVAC) systems; private rooms; private standardized rooms with insulation between the rooms; more absorbent ceiling tile; and "quiet" equipment and technology.

The role of "white noise" in masking other noises is often debated. Of course it is desirable to get rid of as much unnecessary noise as possible first. In the author's experience, even those hospitals that make this attempt still have noise from features such as fans. The fans themselves create a kind of "white noise" that can be a soothing sound, if designed correctly. In situations such as these there probably doesn't need to be more "white noise" in addition to what's already there. The problem with adding "white noise" to cover up undesirable noise (if that noise cannot be or is not designed away) is that it basically adds one additional source of noise to the situation, and that is not ideal. Studies have shown that not only does noise negatively affect sleeping patterns, as might be expected, but "there is strong evidence that noise increases stress in adult patients, for example, heightening blood pressure and heart rate. . . .In sum, the main message from the research review is clear: new hospitals should be much quieter, and effective design strategies for quieting hospitals are available."[8(p.17)]

Scalability, Adaptability, Flexibility

Scalability is the ability to expand or remodel easily so that latent errors are not designed into the building expansion. For example, if radiology does not have adjacent space in which to expand or evolve, major diagnostic technologies could be physically separated in the future, causing potential errors.

Adaptability and flexibility allow spaces to be used for different or evolving services, or functions to be located in different places within the same space, so that latent errors are not created. For example, it could be possible that in the future more procedures (surgical and diagnostic) will be performed in patient rooms, thus minimizing transfers and hand offs.

Many design and construction concepts—everything from open spaces with modular systems to infrastructure requirements to expansion zones that support scalable and adaptable buildings—can be applied to achieve a scalable, adaptable, and flexible health care facility. Specific examples include ceiling heights (floor to floor) to allow for expansion or changes, and wiring for wired or wireless technology that will allow future technology to be easily implemented. Also, locating key services on outside walls creates an infrastructure for future vertical expansion of patient rooms, if necessary.

Visibility of Patients to Staff

In the nineteenth century, it was said that form follows function. In the twenty-first century, it is becoming clear that form shapes function. A well-chosen form helps providers deliver services more efficiently and inexpensively. For example, a pod structure that allows close proximity of caregivers to patients enables nurses to deliver improved quality by allowing them to quickly respond to patient needs and more effectively monitor patient progress.

Unit designs must allow caregivers to be in visual proximity to the patients under their care, as well as accommodate the more traditional orientations of broader-based patient responsibility. This can be accomplished by designing multiple mini-nursing stations throughout the unit, offering alcoves for charting and dictation, and allowing for wall desks either in corridors or patient rooms. Visibility allows staff to see changes in a patient's skin color, observe trouble with breathing, be reminded to change an IV or remember medications, or observe patients attempting to transfer into and out of bed without assistance. Timely help can decrease these patient safety risks.

Lighting can also help improve patient visibility to staff. The light source can change a patient's appearance, causing unnecessary concerns about potential changes in the patient's medical condition. For example, if a patient in a room with natural light is transferred to a room with incandescent light, the patient may look more yellow or jaundiced. Proper lighting is necessary to conduct an accurate patient assessment. Natural light versus other lighting sources is also an important consideration. A study conducted at Montefiore University Hospital in Pittsburgh showed that patients in rooms with greater natural light took less pain medication, resulting in a 21% reduction of drug costs as compared to equally ill patients in rooms with less natural light.[9]

Additional design features to enhance visibility of patients include windows in alcove doors, which allow caregivers to conveniently check on patients without disturbing them; patient care areas wired for cameras; and a family area in every patient room to encourage family members to stay with patients for a longer period.

In addition to lighting, many mechanical, electrical, and plumbing changes that are different from a traditional hospital design can be incorporated into new design. Noise, information close to the patient, and fatigue are all affected by mechanical, electrical, and plumbing decisions. For example, fans in most hospitals create a lot of noise but they can be designed to produce fewer decibels. Wiring plans can allow for computers to be located near the patient and be available to caregivers.

Patients Involved with Their Care

Keeping patients informed gives them the opportunity to participate in shared decision making with physicians and may help patients better articulate their individual views and preferences to physicians and nurses. During a hospital stay, keeping patients and family members informed can also potentially reduce error. Patients or their family members could receive a daily schedule of prescribed medication and treatments. They should be encouraged to verify this information with the caregivers administering the medication or treatment. For example, they could ask whether all caregivers have washed their hands.

Ideally, every patient area could have a designated "family" section that is distinct from the "caregiver" section to encourage family members to stay with the patient. Various features that could be included

---

According to the Center for Health Design, exposure to daylight does the following:

- Reduces depression among patients with seasonal affective disorder and bipolar depression
- Decreases length of stay in hospitals
- Improves sleep and circadian rhythms
- Lessens agitation among dementia patients and eases pain
- Improves adjustment to night-shift work among staff

Source: Joseph A.: *The Impact of Light on Outcomes in Healthcare Settings*. The Center for Health Design. Aug. 2006. http://www.healthdesign.org/research/reports/documents/CHD_Issue_Paper2.pdf (accessed May 30, 2007).

in a patient room are a foldout couch, a desk with access to the Internet and other power sources, and storage closets for patient and family members' belongings. Space with chairs would be a desirable feature in an outpatient room; standing areas could be provided in procedure rooms. A large window would help create a well-lit and inviting space. In addition, a television and portable computer stand could be made available for use by patients and families as well as caregivers, so that patients and families can be fully informed of medication and treatment plans. Locating a sink with liquid soap and alcohol-based hand rub dispensers in direct view of the patients could help caregivers ensure compliance with hand washing.

Standardization

Care standardization substantially impacts the basic consequences of organizational factors to reduce medical errors and improve quality. Standardization has been documented as an important strategy in human factors design.[10–12] It can reduce reliance on short-term memory and allow those unfamiliar with a given process or design to use it safely. Much of the work in human factors focuses on improving the human-systems interface by designing better systems and processes. Examples include standardization of patient rooms, treatment areas, equipment, and procedures. Standardization of the facility and room design—from the location of the outlets to bed controls to which cupboard to store latex gloves to the charting process, even to switches on light fixtures, down to the smallest detail—all have an impact on behavior.

In *The Psychology of Everyday Things*, Norman talks about design novelty, stating, "Users don't want each new design to use a different method for a task. Users need standardization."[10] Specific examples to consider in facility standardization include the following:

- Truly standardized patient rooms
- Standardized emergency exam rooms, postrecovery rooms, ambulatory/diagnostic exam rooms, and admission/observation rooms
- Standardized locations of all gases throughout the facility
- Standardized IVs, beds, monitors, and all equipment
- Standardized medication systems and other care systems
- Standardized mechanical, electrical, and plumbing systems

Automation Where Possible

In its 2001 report, *Crossing the Quality Chasm: A New Health System for the 21st Century*, the Institute of Medicine (IOM) identifies information technology (IT) solutions as a necessary component of improving patient safety. Many errors occur because clinicians do not have access to complete and accurate patient information, and because they are often responsible for remembering large amounts of knowledge such as drug-to-drug interactions for a large number of medications.

When designing a new health care facility, technology planning should begin on day 1 of the design process. If possible, ongoing assessment of the type and frequency of errors within the existing institution will help determine specific technological needs and set priorities. To facilitate the decision process create a list of the IT systems needed or desired and characterize the systems according to their relationship to one another and their impact on patient safety, financial investment, implementation time, facility design, and operation. The financial investment should reflect the total cost of ownership, including costs for purchase, implementation, maintenance, and staff support.

Safe hospitals of the future will be highly digitized, minimizing human touches of data and providing robust decision support. Another future safety goal will be providing complete and accurate information at the point of service to multiple providers simultaneously. Design features include proper wiring for current and future needs, and wired and wireless technologies strategically located throughout the facility. Some examples include computers, radiology screens, monitors, uninterruptible power systems, and information infrastructure. Which technologies are chosen and how they are used (for example, nurse call systems, security, materials, radio frequency identification devices [RFID], and bar coding) could have significant impact on room design and adjacencies.

Minimizing Fatigue

Research has identified fatigue as a contributing factor of human error. Studies have shown that fatigue has a negative impact on alertness, mood, and psychomotor and cognitive performance, all of which can have an impact on patient safety.[13] Shift work and, in certain circumstances, long hours and increased work loads are inevitable in patient care. As a result, minimizing fatigue is a complex issue in hospitals that requires a comprehensive approach. In facility design, this could mean minimizing the distances staff must travel between patient rooms, nursing stations, and treatment areas. Decisions could affect not only the number of patient rooms per floor but also vertical and horizontal adjacencies of departments.

The use of technology can increase the efficiency of work loads and reduce reliance on short-term memory and thought processes. One example is the computerized tube transport system that can either eliminate or significantly reduce the need for staff to hand-deliver laboratory specimens, blood products, or medical supplies—all of which can increase efficiency.

As previously discussed, noise reduction can also minimize fatigue in hospital staff and patients. Several design features can be implemented to minimize noise for patients and staff. Insulated walls and standardized, private patient rooms in which head walls are not shared will reduce the transfer of noise between rooms. Triple-glazed windows will reduce outside noise. Noise from inside the hospital can be reduced by eliminating overhead paging, installing absorbent floor coverings (carpet, rubber) and ceiling tile, and using "quiet" equipment and technology such as HVAC systems and paper towel dispensers.

Immediate Accessibility of Information, Close to the Point of Service

Research has shown that lack of knowledge and information can lead to errors.[11,14] As stated earlier, two significant causes of adverse drug events (ADEs) and potential ADEs are lack of drug knowledge and inadequate availability of patient information. New technologies can help physicians and other caregivers with complex cognitive tasks such as diagnosis and treatment by providing "real-time" medical information. These technologies include the Internet, computer-based patient records, and clinical decision support systems.

In addition to technological solutions, other examples for improving the immediate accessibility of information close to the point of service include charting alcoves directly adjacent to patient rooms, providing caregivers easy access to patient charts without disrupting the patient; and surgery operating rooms that are equipped with large boards or monitors displaying patient information and scheduled procedures, verifying physician instructions and showing the patient's chart and medical records.

Minimizing Patient Transfers/Hand Offs

Transferring puts patients and staff in a vulnerable position in which patients or staff could be harmed and causes disruption for ill patients. A transfer from a patient room usually involves multiple transfers. A patient is transferred to surgery or to radiology, transferred to a table in both locations, and then is transferred to the patient bed again. These transfers often involve hand offs: nurse to transporter to radiology tech to transporter to nurse, creating the potential for error or harm. Many other hand offs involving multiple caregivers occur in a facility, such as physician to nurse to nurse to radiology tech to lab techs, and so on, in high-risk circumstances. These conditions are ripe for error.

Minimizing patient transfers/hand offs or minimizing the risk of harm when transferring patients have many facility design implications. It is safer to design services to come to the patient, not the reverse. This design needs to be adaptable so that future services can come *to* the patient. Potential errors resulting from transfers and hand offs can be minimized by having lifts in every care area in the hospital, barcoding for patient identification, and electronic medical records (EMRs), so that complete and accurate information is available for caregivers at the point of service where hand offs occur.

Space should be sized so that as many services as possible can be provided in the patient room.

The Significance of Active Failures and Their Impact on Safety Design

An active failure is an unintentional mistake, a failure of execution—something that occurs when the plan is correct but the actions fail to go as planned. Active failures typically occur at the point of harm (adverse events), such as forgetting to check a medication before giving it. The active failures on which a health care organization focuses attention should be based on the organization's own database of sentinel events, adverse events, medical errors, and near misses; national databases such as the Sentinel Events Database from The Joint Commission; and the report, *Serious Reportable Events in Healthcare*, issued by the National Quality Forum. The facility design process should focus on preventing the occurrence of these active failures (such as the nine identified by the National Learning Lab and shown in Table 4-6, left).

Table 4-6. Active Failures

1. Operative/postoperative complications/infections
2. Inpatient suicides
3. Incorrect tube—incorrect connector—incorrect hole placement events/oxygen cylinder hazards
4. Medication error–related events
5. Wrong-site surgery events
6. Deaths of patients in restraints
7. Transfusion-related events
8. Patient falls
9. MRI hazards

Operative/Postoperative Complications/ Infections

One of the most harmful and costly active failures

is operative/postoperative complications and infections. Postoperative infections, surgical wounds accidentally opening, and other often-preventable complications lead to more than 32,000 U.S. hospital deaths and more than $9 billion in extra costs annually, according to The Joint Commission.[15] The Centers for Disease Control and Prevention estimates that nearly two million patients in U.S. hospitals each year develop an infection. Approximately 90,000 of these patients die as a result of their infection.[15]

Facility design considerations that address this problem include placing sinks in every patient care area, which encourages care providers to wash their hands in view of the patient; using high-efficiency particulate air (HEPA) filters and ultraviolet lights in all public areas and in key patient care areas to reduce airborne pathogens; eliminating window blinds to reduce condensation; designing single-patient rooms; using air flow in patient rooms (modified "laminar flow"); and standardizing and making prominently visible the location of sanitizer dispensers. Another possibility is to install a separate air system, with HEPA and ultraviolet filters, for the emergency room waiting area. In addition, the number of times the air is removed and returned (exchanges per hour) can be increased, particularly in the surgical areas.

Mechanical systems can be designed to create positive air flow, negative air flow, or laminar air flow into hospital rooms, depending on the requirements of the various rooms. Negative pressure isolation rooms keep a flow of air into the room, to prevent contaminants and pathogens from reaching surrounding areas. This is commonly used in tuberculosis (TB) rooms, because the infectivity of TB is extremely high, and these rooms are essential to protect health workers and other patients. Positive pressure isolation rooms maintain a flow of air out of the room, to protect the patient from contaminants and pathogens that might otherwise come in. This is often used in HIV rooms and rooms for patients with other types of immunodeficiency; for these patients, it is very important to prevent contact with any pathogens, including even common fungi and bacteria that may be harmless to healthy people. Laminar flows are very even, smooth, low-velocity airflows that enter a room, flow over the patient, and exit on the other side of the room; they are used in "clean rooms" or surgical suites where high-quality ventilation is critical. But laminar flows can be expensive and difficult to achieve because furnishings, vents, and other features may create turbulence. St. Joseph's Hospital applied the concept of laminar flow to the patient rooms, calling their system a "modified laminar flow": Intake was through a vent near the sink, air flowed over the foot of the patient's bed, and went out through a vent near the family area of the patient room (and all the air in all the patient areas was HEPA–filtered).

Inpatient Suicides

Inpatient suicides cause a great deal of distress to relatives of the patient as well as caregivers. Research indicates there are approximately 30,000 suicides in the United States per year, approximately 6% of which occur in hospitals.[16] Because of the challenges encountered with predicting suicide risk, facility design considerations are an important component of inpatient suicide prevention. Patient rooms should be designed for maximum visibility through cameras or glass in alcove doors, and by providing a comfortable space for family members to remain with the patient for longer periods. Patient rooms should be equipped with breakaway curtain rods and "suicide proof" showerheads (showerheads that are designed so that items cannot hang from them, rather they slide off) or other comparable equipment. Windows should be nonoperable so that a patient cannot jump from them. Special attention should be given to ensuring that sharp objects or other harmful items are not stored in the patient room.

Incorrect Tube—Incorrect Connector—Incorrect Hole Placement Events/Oxygen Cylinder Hazards

Most types of incorrect tube/incorrect connector/incorrect hole placement events/oxygen cylinder hazards are inadvertent mix-ups of gases or tubes being attached to the wrong locations. Facility design elements to consider include common storage of gases, color coding, standardizing the headwall location of gases throughout the hospital, and using different-size connectors for the different gases and tube connections—a "forcing function" that prevents inadvertent mix-ups of gases or tube connections.

Medication Error–Related Events

Medication-related errors are one of the most common types of errors occurring in hospitals. The IOM report *To Err Is Human: Building a Safer Health System* cited studies showing that in 1993, approximately 7,000 deaths were attributable to medication errors and that 1 out of every 854 inpatient hospital deaths resulted from a medication error. The IOM estimates that increased hospital costs resulting from preventable ADEs affecting inpatients are approximately $2 billion for the nation as a whole.[17] A recent report from the IOM, *Preventing Medication Errors* (2006), that studied data from adults in the United States who take prescription drugs, over-the-counter medications, and supplements showed that one third of these adults take five or more medications. This increases the chance for medication error. The report provides advice on reducing medication errors and offers prevention strategies.[18]

Studies have shown that technology can have a significant impact on patient safety and quality of care. Facility designs should make certain that proper wiring/cabling is included in all areas of the hospital where medication can be dispensed or delivered, with wireless and wired capability for computers and other technologies such as bar coding. In addition, a pneumatic tube system should be installed in all central areas where medication will be dispensed or ordered. Technology plans should include an integrated system consisting of EMRs, decision support, computerized prescriber order entry (CPOE), bar coding, and an automated pharmacy system. Design plans to reduce medication errors include single-patient rooms where medications will be stored in locked containers, and verifying medications using bar-coding technology when medications are delivered.

Wrong-Site Surgery

Wrong-site surgery has received widespread media attention in recent years. Although efforts to address this problem have increased, it remains a significant concern. Facility design considerations that will complement the Joint Commission's Universal Protocol for Preventing Wrong Site, Wrong Procedure, Wrong Person Surgery™ and other process recommendations include standardizing operating room suites, installing proper lighting, and installing cable for accessing digital images and photographs of surgery sites along with x-rays, so that "reverse" readings do not occur and patient information is always available.

Deaths of Patients in Restraints

Despite efforts to reduce restraint use, preventing deaths resulting from restraint use continues to be an area of concern in health care. Through December 31, 2006, almost 4% of all sentinel events reported to The Joint Commission were restraint-related deaths.[19] Facility design considerations to reduce the risk of restraint deaths include providing a comfortable space for family members to stay with the patient to provide the patient with additional support and comfort; increasing the visibility of patients through cameras or windows in alcove doors so that staff can provide increased or continuous observation can help to minimize the need for restraints; providing space in the caregiver or family areas for someone to remain with the patient for longer periods, which can also help reduce the need for restraints.

Transfusion-Related Events

The implementation of an integrated technology system for laboratories/blood banks is key to reducing potential errors and adverse outcomes in the blood transfusion process. Tube systems, EMRs, bar coding, CPOE, decision support, and automated lab systems can reduce the likelihood of transfusion-related events. Proper wiring and computer location are some of the facility features necessary to implement the technology.

Patient Falls

Despite research on identifying risk factors and developing fall prevention programs, patient falls remain a common adverse event. Risk factors have been identified to aid health care providers in identifying patients who have a greater likelihood of falling. These risk factors include altered mental status, decreased mobility, history of falls, toileting needs (where assistance is needed, or incontinence), medications, age, and other factors such as dizziness or length of hospitalization.

Falls often occur at night as patients attempt to get out of bed because they are disoriented or need to use the restroom. In a Joint Commission review of 22 cases of fatal falls, 13 occurred in general hospitals, with 1 occurring in a psychiatric unit. Most of the patients were older than 85 years of age. Approximately one third of the cases involved the patient falling from a bed. Other falls occurred while the patient was walking or using the bathroom, or moving or being transferred from a commode, gurney, or chair.[20]

Facility design considerations that can help reduce patient falls include enhancing visibility of patients to staff and creating or using existing technology to "catch" high-risk patients before they leave their beds, thus eliminating potential falls. Facility considerations include the following:

- Bathrooms located near the head of the bed, so that patients always have a handrail to hold onto and no open space to cross
- Alcove door with windows, so that medical/surgical patients are generally visible to staff
- Beds that can be lowered close to the floor to minimize fall risk
- Softer flooring, such as carpet and rubber
- "Infrared" technologies that can send an emergency call to the nurse call system when patients leave their bed and turn on lights
- Wiring for digital cameras that could observe patients with a high risk of falling

MRI Hazards

Magnetic metal objects are still brought into the MRI with some frequency, causing death and harm to patients. One source is the patient's own metals, such as a pacemaker. Design features that can reduce

MRI hazards include using a three-room process to enter, locating connections for gases in rooms, color-coding all stretchers and wheelchairs as to magnetic or nonmagnetic, and using a handheld metal detector to check staff before entering. Because this is an active failure, process changes will have a more significant impact than facility changes. All active failures and latent conditions are impacted by process changes.

Clearly, facility design that eliminates latent conditions and active failures as much as possible will have an impact on the overall safety of patients within that facility.

References

1. Voelker R.: "Pebbles" cast ripples in health care design. *JAMA* 286(14):1701–1702, 2001.

2. DeRosier J., et al.: Using health care failure mode and effect analysis: The VA National Center for Patient Safety's prospective risk analysis system. *Jt Comm J Qual Improv* 28(5):248–267, 2002.

3. Stamatis D.H.: *Failure Mode and Effects Analysis.* Milwaukee: American Society of Quality Press, 1995.

4. *Potential Failure Mode and Effects Analysis (FMEA): Reference Manual,* 3rd ed. Detroit: General Motors Corporation, 2001.

5. de Jong R.G., et al.: *Proceedings of the 8th International Congress on Noise as a Public Health Problem.* Rotterdam, the Netherlands, Jun. 29–Jul. 3, 2003 (Foundation ICBEN 2003 Congress, Schiedam, the Netherlands, 2003).

6. Murthy V.S., et al.: Detrimental effects of noise on anaesthetists. *Can J Anaesth* 42(7):608–611, 1995.

7. Berens R.J.: Noise in the pediatric intensive care unit. *J Intensive Care Medicine* 14(3):118–129, 1999.

8. Ulrich R., Zimring C.: The role of the physical environment in the hospital of the 21st century: A once-in-a-lifetime opportunity. Report to The Center for Health Design, for the Designing for the 21st Century Hospital Project, 2004.

9. Walch J.M., et al.: The effect of sunlight on post-operative analgesic medication usage: A prospective study of spinal surgery patients. *Psychosom Med* 67(1):156–163, 2005.

10. Norman D.A.: *The Psychology of Everyday Things.* New York: Basic Books, 1988.

11. Reason J.T.: *Human Error.* Cambridge: Cambridge University Press, 1990.

12. Liker J.K.: *The Toyota Way: 14 Management Principles from the World's Greatest Manufacturer.* New York: McGraw-Hill, 2004.

13. Jha A.K., Duncan B.W., Bates D.W.: Fatigue, sleepiness, and medical errors. In Shojania K.G., et al. (eds.): *Making Health Care Safer: Critical Analysis of Patient Safety Practices.* Rockville, MD: Agency for Healthcare Research and Quality, 2002.

14. Leape L.L.: Error in medicine. *JAMA* 272(23):1851–1857, 1994.

15. Joint Commission on Accreditation of Healthcare Organizations: Infection control related sentinel events. *Sentinel Event Alert* 28, Jan. 22, 2003. Available at http://www.jointcommission.org/SentinelEvents/SentinelEventAlert/sea_28.htm.

16. Busch K.A., Fawcett M.D., Jacobs D.G.: Clinical correlates of inpatient suicides. *J Clin Psychiatry* 64(1):14–19, 2003.

17. Institute of Medicine: *To Err Is Human: Building a Safer Health System.* Washington, DC: National Academy Press, 1999.

18. Institute of Medicine: *Preventing Medication Errors: Quality Chasm Series.* Washington, DC: National Academy Press, 2006.

19. Joint Commission on Accreditation of Healthcare Organizations: *Sentinel Event Statistics: As of March 31, 2006.* http://www.jointcommission.org/NR/rdonlyres/74540565-4D0F-4992-863E-8F9E949E6B56/0/se_stats_0331.pdf (accessed Jun. 15, 2007).

20. Joint Commission on Accreditation of Healthcare Organizations: Fatal falls: lesson for the future. *Sentinel Event Alert* 14, Jul. 14, 2000. Available at http://www.jointcommission.org/SentinelEvents/SentinelEventAlert/sea_14.htm.

Chapter 5
Using the Facility Design Process to Enhance a Safety Culture

"Advances in patient safety, especially when involving the management of human error, depend upon our collective ability to learn from our mistakes." (David Marx, J.D., *"Patient Safety and the 'Just Culture': A Primer for Health Care Executives."* Prepared for Columbia University under a grant provided by the National Heart, Lung, and Blood Institute, New York: 2001, p. 3.)

How can a patient safety culture be created or enhanced as a result of a new focus on patient safety in facility design? Because patient safety is an integral part of the delivery of quality care, achieving an acceptable standard of patient safety requires that all health care settings develop comprehensive patient safety systems, including both a culture of safety and organizational supports for safety processes. A key aspect of a patient safety system is a culture that encourages clinicians, patients, and others to be vigilant in (1) identifying potential or actual errors, (2) taking appropriate steps to prevent and mitigate harm, and (3) disclosing appropriate information on errors that do occur to facilitate learning and the redesign of care processes. As noted above, safe care settings are ones that have an adequate information infrastructure to provide clinicians and patients with immediate access to health information. But other organizational supports are needed as well, including trained professionals with expertise in safety, and well-designed reporting systems for near misses and adverse events.[1]

James Reason defines culture as "Shared values (what is important) and beliefs (how things work) that interact with an organization's structures and control systems to produce behavioral norms (the way we do things around here)." Reason says safety culture has different parts—an informed culture, a reporting culture, a just culture, a flexible culture, and a learning culture. He also believes that a safety culture can be engineered, in the social sense.[2]

Another expert in the field, Kenneth W. Kizer, M.D., developed his own list of the characteristics of a culture of safety; they are shown in Table 5-1 (below).

Table 5-1. Kizer's Culture of Safety

1. Acknowledgment of risk and responsibility for risk reduction
2. Errors recognized and valued as opportunities for improvement
3. Nonpunitive and safe environment; freedom from fear
4. Honest and open communication with confidentiality of information
5. Mechanisms for reporting and learning
6. Mechanisms for restitution and compensation for injuries
7. Organizational commitment, structure, and accountability

Source: Kizer K.W.: Large system change and a culture of safety. In *Enhancing Patient Safety and Reducing Errors*. Chicago: National Patient Safety Foundation, 1999. Used with permission.

Table 5-2: Safety Culture Recommendations

1. Shared values and beliefs about safety within the organization
2. Always anticipating active failures
3. Informed employees and medical staff
4. Culture of reporting
5. Learning culture
6. "Just" culture
7. Blame-free environment recognizing human fallibility
8. Physician teamwork
9. Culture of continuous improvement
10. Empowering families to participate in care of patients
11. Informed and active patients

The National Learning Lab's safety culture recommendations are shown in Table 5-2 (page 60).

The importance of a safety culture in creating a safe health care experience cannot be underestimated. If safety is important to an organization and if an organization does things with safety in mind, a safer experience will result for patients and staff. The systems of an organization are highly influenced by its culture or are a reflection of its culture. Equally, an organization's culture influences how facilities—with their equipment and technology—are developed. In other words, the influence moves both ways. One can use facility development processes to influence culture, while at the same time the environment itself can influence culture. Facilities, systems, and culture are highly interrelated concepts.

The facility development process, that is, the process to remodel a health care facility or develop a new one, can create, change, or enhance culture. System redesign focused on safety will also enhance the culture of patient safety. By having patient safety as the guiding principle and "engineering" that principle, the culture of patient safety will be enhanced. Two important components that will help accomplish this are the commitment of top management and involvement of staff who are providing care (*see* Chapter 9 for more on this subject).

Shared Values and Beliefs About Safety Within the Organization

The development of shared values and beliefs is one of the most important—and difficult—elements of a safety culture. Without recognizing human error and the current processes and facilities that create environments where significant errors occur, leading to patient harm, why would caregivers focus on safety in design?

Recognizing that everyone is human and will make mistakes is a difficult reality for health care providers. Perfection is correlated to competence; mistakes are correlated to incompetence. Instead of being dedicated to creating facilities and systems that catch mistakes, or to create barriers and environments so that mistakes are less likely to occur, health care providers are trained to dedicate themselves to demanding individual perfection. The disciplinary policies of the health care industry as a whole, and the education of professionals who practice in the industry, reinforce the emphasis on individual perfection as a goal.

Chapter 1 discussed the types and root causes of errors, lapses, slips, and mistakes that humans make. But to recognize that everyday many errors will be made is difficult for health care providers to internalize. It's as though someone assumes that he or she *will* make a mistake at work, possibly causing harm. Most people would assume they would do a "good" job, meaning they will make no mistakes. In a way, people have to be convinced they are "failures" to accept the concept of human error. The perfectionist model leads to disciplinary behavior that punishes employees for making mistakes that might be the result of human error. It has been said that the single greatest impediment to error prevention in the medical industry is punishing people for making mistakes.[3]

To develop an organization focused on facility design for safety, one needs to understand human error and recognize the current error rates and harm. Without that, there is no motivation to change. Some strategies that can help develop shared values within an organization are storytelling (particularly about incidents that occurred within the organization) anonymous reporting surveys, and open discussions about the human condition.

Informed Employees and Medical Staff, Culture of Reporting, Learning Culture, Just Culture, Blame-Free Environment Recognizing Human Fallibility, Culture of Continuous Improvement

A blame-free environment must recognize that human fallibility, reporting, learning, continuous improvement, and just cultures are intertwined concepts. They need to become part of a working environment that employees and medical staff can understand and be committed to. The concept of a just culture is the foundation for all others. A just culture recognizes human error and justified at-risk behavior and does not punish it; rather, it punishes what is called reckless behavior. Stealing narcotics would be an example of reckless behavior.

Recognizing human fallibility leads to a blame-free environment for mistakes that are caused by human error. What meaning does discipline have for someone who has made a mistake caused by human error? If an organization is going to develop a facility in which human error is minimized, it needs to have the reporting to know what conditions and processes need to change. To ensure reporting of human error, an organization cannot discipline employees for human error, because many, if not most, employees will not report an error that leads to a disciplinary action. The underreporting that typically occurs in a hospital is material. Therefore, it follows that if a reporting culture is created and human error is not disciplined, the organization also needs to act on the reports received. If a report does not result in change, why would employees waste their time reporting?

A learning culture needs to be created so that appropriate environmental and process changes are pursued to minimize the potential of human error or catch the errors and turn them into near misses so that patients are not harmed. This leads to informed employees and medical staff who are committed to continually improving processes and facilities and managing at-risk behavior to improve patient safety.

A number of concepts need to be accepted to develop a just culture, including the belief that to err is human, to "drift" is human, risk is everywhere, safety is a value, and everyone is accountable for safety. Chapter 1 addressed the concept, "to err is human." A related concept is "human drift," which refers to the notion that, as we become comfortable with a risky circumstance, we drift away from the safe zone. For example, drivers may gradually combine driving with other activities, such as talking on a cell phone, taking notes, driving with their knees, and speeding. In other words, people normalize risky behavior and assess the risk versus the utility of the risk. Risk is everywhere, especially in hospitals. For example, an operating room has inherent risks but the social value is worth the risk. Everyone in a hospital is accountable for safety; that means always being on the outlook for risks that lead to harm, accepting human fallibility, and taking responsibility for system design and behavior choices to support safe practices.[4]

Managers have three strategies to improve safety:

1. Focus on safety in design for facilities with their technology and equipment (facility development).
2. Create safe processes (the processes that people use to do their work).
3. Manage safety culture (for example, at-risk behaviors).

If an employee makes an error considered to be a human error, management's response should be to console that employee and investigate and implement system or facility changes to minimize or mitigate the possibility of that error recurring. If an employee makes an error as a result of taking a justified risk (that is, the employee had good intentions but did not realize what the consequences would be), management should counsel the employee about his or her behavior and determine what system or facility changes should occur.

For example, a lab technician decides not to label a tube of blood in front of the patient at the patient's bedside (per the hospital's policy), because the patient complained of the bright light. In addition, the lab technician decides to label the tube at the nurse's station because it is the last tube to label and she has only one label left for the tube. A nurse then mistakenly exchanges the tube of blood with a blood sample the nurse had drawn from a different patient. The mislabeled blood leads to the wrong blood being given to a patient, who has a negative reaction. The lab technician did not intend for the harm to happen and did not realize it could happen as a result of not following the hospital's policy. She was trying to be patient centered. Such at-risk behavior needs to be counseled so that circumstances such as this do not happen again. In addition, the process and/or facility need to be evaluated to see if any changes could have minimized or eliminated the possibility of the lab technician being placed in the position in which she made the mistake.

On the other hand, if a caregiver exhibits risky behavior that he or she knows could lead to harm, disciplinary action should result. For example, a physician in the operating room drops an instrument and asks for a replacement, but the replacement instrument is not readily available. In frustration and under time pressure, the physician picks up the instrument from the floor and continues surgery. In this case, the physician knows the sterile field requirement, but he knowingly takes a risk out of frustration, not for any reason of "social utility." In instances such as this, disciplinary action would be required.

Initiating a just culture is not always easy. Caregivers may be concerned at times that disciplinary action is not taken against human error (for example, if they see all human error as avoidable and/or intentional). One way of encouraging a just culture is to incorporate it into the system of performance evaluation for caregivers, including physicians. For example, the Quality Committee of the medical staff

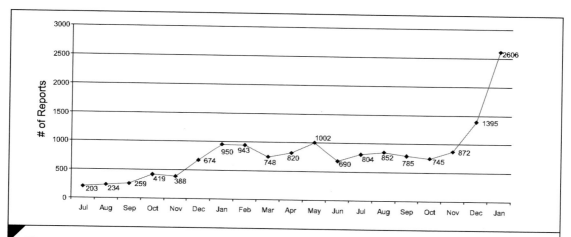

Figure 5-1. Monthly Medication Safety Reports, 2002–2004, St. Joseph's Hospital, West Bend, Wisconsin.
This figure shows an increase in monthly medication reports over a two-year period.

Source: St. Joseph's Hospital, West Bend, WI. Used with permission.

could change its approach based on the information staff receives about a just culture. Disciplinary policies could be evaluated to match the concepts of a just culture. Also, the hospital's management team could evaluate employee behavior using the concepts of a just culture. In another step toward a just culture, employees and management could set up a confidential and anonymous reporting process, as outlined in Chapter 3, making sure that the reports include errors, near misses, and adverse events. The results of such reporting have been shown to be dramatic and encouraging. For example, since medication error reports began to be used at St. Joseph's Hospital in West Bend, Wisconsin, the number of reports each month grew steadily from a baseline of approximately 250 before October 2002 to 2,602 in January 2004 (*see* Figure 5-1, above).

Another strategy for improved safety is to create a checklist of active failures and patient safety design principles. Each employee and department should be asked to complete a checklist that documents the design impact on patient safety. *See* Figure 5-2 on pages 62–66 for a sample checklist.

Executive walk-arounds focused on safety can be also initiated to educate managers on safety issues and employee concerns. (During walk-arounds, senior leaders walk around the organization, speaking with front-line staff to learn about safety issues so as to bring about improvements and cultural change.) Priorities for capital expenditures are also being influenced by a focus on patient safety. The recognition of the interplay between technology, physical plant, and equipment to maximize safety is critical and enhances the culture of patient safety.

Educating physicians and staff about the human condition, the nature of error, latent conditions, active failures, and the brainstorming process around patient safety design principles will contribute to creating a safe environment for patients and staff. A better reporting culture is enhanced by this focus on safety, which in turn leads to an improved learning culture influenced by the underlying just culture.

Guiding Principles Checklist

☐ **Visibility of Patients to Staff**
Comments:_____
_____
_____

Have you incorporated this principle into your department design?
☐ Yes
☐ No

☐ Standardization
Examples: ED Common Equipment
Same Room Design
Standardization of Gases
Comments:_____
_____
_____

Have you incorporated this principle into your department design?
☐ Yes
☐ No

☐ **Automate Where Possible**
Examples: Bar Coding Medications
Tube System/Delivery of Materials
Dumb Waiter/Elevator Adjacencies
Centralized Scheduling
Bedside Registration
Materials Management Software
Future Electronic Medical Record
Future Electronic Prescriber Order Entry
Future Filmless Radiology
Nurse Call System
Comments:_____
_____
_____

Have you incorporated this principle into your department design?
☐ Yes
☐ No

(continued on page 63)

Figure 5-2. Guiding Principles Checklist.
This checklist can be used as hospitals consider how precarious events and patient safety design principles affect the "safe by design" process.

☐ **Guiding Principles Checklist (continued)**

☐ **Scalability, Adaptability, Flexibility**
Examples: Expansion plans, if needed. Ability to remodel easily.
Comments:_____
_____
_____

Have you incorporated this principle into your department design?
☐ Yes
☐ No

☐ **Immediate Accessibility of Information, Close to the Point of Service**
Comments:_____
_____
_____

Have you incorporated this principle into your department design?
☐ Yes
☐ No

☐ **Noise Reduction**
Examples: Carpet. No Overhead Paging.
Comments:_____
_____
_____

Have you incorporated this principle into your department design?
☐ Yes
☐ No

☐ **Patients Involved with Their Care**
Example: Bedside computers.
Comments:_____
_____
_____

Have you incorporated this principle into your department design?
☐ Yes
☐ No

(continued on page 64)

63

Guiding Principles Checklist (continued)

☐ **FMEA of Departments and Department Rooms**
Risk analysis and risk reduction recommendations
Comments:_____
_____
_____

Have you incorporated this principle into your department design?
☐ Yes
☐ No
• Education to be provided

☐ **Design for the Vulnerable Patient**
Design around the vulnerable part of a person's stay.
Comments:_____
_____
_____

Have you incorporated this principle into your department design?
☐ Yes
☐ No

☐ **Human Factors Review**
Examples: Equipment design relates to human behavior to minimize error.
　　　　　Is room designed so mistakes are eliminated or minimized?
Comments:_____
_____
_____

Have you incorporated this principle into your department design?
☐ Yes
☐ No
• Education on concepts to be provided

☐ **Minimize Fatigue**
Comments:_____
_____
_____

Have you incorporated this principle into your department design?
☐ Yes
☐ No

(continued on page 65)

Guiding Principles Checklist (continued)

☐ **Precarious Events**

Examples: Operative/Postoperative Complications/Infection
Inpatient Suicides
Correct Tube–Correct Connector–Correct Hole
Deaths Related to Surgery at Wrong Site
Oxygen Cylinder Hazard
Events Relating to Medication Errors
Deaths of Patients in Restraints
Transfusion-Related Events
Patient Falls
MRI Hazards

Comments:_____
_____
_____

Have you incorporated this principle into your department design?
☐ Yes
☐ No

☐ **Efficient**

Have we designed to most effectively use staff time? Are we duplicating functions between departments?

Comments:_____
_____
_____

Have you incorporated this principle into your department design?
☐ Yes
☐ No

☐ **Healing Environment**

Examples: Noise Reduction
Calming Environment
Lighting
Viewing Nature
Connection to Nature

Comments:_____
_____
_____

Have you incorporated this principle into your department design?
☐ Yes
☐ No

(continued on page 66)

Guiding Principles Checklist (continued)

☐ **Advanced Technology**
  Example: Staff friendly.
        Do we have equipment and technology that maximize safety?
  Comments:_____
  _____
  _____

  Have you incorporated this principle into your department design?
  ☐ Yes
  ☐ No

  List Major Process Assumptions as Part of Design
  _____
  _____
  _____

  Identify Changes from Current Processes (How/What Other Departments Are Affected)
  _____
  _____
  _____

  Design Assumptions:
  Separation of public/patient/service traffic
  Onstage, offstage concept
  Breakrooms for geographic areas, not department specific

Empowering Families to Participate in Care of Patients/Informed and Active Patients

Empowering families to participate in care can also change safety culture. Historically, information regarding medication use is given verbally to patients and families. Instead, patients and their families can be given medication administration records. This change creates more questions (and a resulting education) about patients' medications, which then leads to more prepared families when their family members returned home. It also adds another barrier against potential adverse medication events. Patients and families are educated about the five "rights of medication": right patient, right drug, right dose, right route, and right time. This helps them verify and catch misses and mistakes, thus creating fewer adverse medication events. Another example is hand washing, an essential way to lower infections: educating and involving patients and families in the importance of hand washing increases overall compliance with hand washing.

Developing a patient safety culture is a critical element of safety by design, and is therefore critical to the goal of improving patient safety in a hospital. Using all the tools that have been discussed in this chapter, plus others, can help hospitals create and enhance a patient safety culture as a result of a new focus on patient safety in facility design.

References

1.   Institute of Medicine: *Patient Safety: Achieving a New Standard for Care.* Washington, DC: National Academy Press, 2004.

2.   Reason J.: *Managing the Risks of Organizational Accidents.* Aldershot, UK: Ashgate Publishing, 1997.

3.   Leape L.L.: Error in medicine. *JAMA* 272(23):1851–1857, 1994.

4.   David Marx, JD, has a research and consulting practice focusing on the management of human error through the integration of systems engineering, human factors, and the law.

Chapter 6
Safe by Design: An Architect's Perspective

by Thomas K. Wallen, AIA

"Health care planning and design professionals stand without excuse. We are able to design health care facilities which compel the delivery of safe, error-free care." (Tom Wallen)

An Architect's Introduction

As an architect experienced in hospital design, I was once asked, "Does the design of a hospital affect a caregiver's ability to provide safe care?" Intuitively, I knew the answer was, "Yes, of course it does." However, the ability of caregivers to provide safe care has not traditionally been a major focus of the design process. Yes, safe care is always the chief aim when providing health care. But it was assumed that the designing and building of an efficient healing environment would automatically result in safe health care. Never before, to my knowledge, had the health care design process been completely focused on creating a hospital that was "safe by design." But the idea that my design projects had included latent conditions that supported and possibly promoted active failures (medical errors) was unexpected and unacceptable to me. Therefore, I chose to accept the challenge of designing a hospital that would be a healing environment, and one that, as a result of its design, would help eliminate medical error.

Upon examination of the traditional design process that exposes latent conditions that lead to design failures, the following questions arose:

- Why do we spend so little time designing the operational processes functioning within the hospital before designing the building?
- Why do we delay decisions regarding the design of a patient room, exam room, or operating room to a time in the process that makes it impossible or at best costly and time consuming to address?
- Why do we deny hospital staff the opportunity to physically explore through life-size mock-ups the redundant spaces that will be repeated 50 to 100 or more times in the design of their hospital?
- What are other industries doing to improve quality and eliminate errors, and will their methods work effectively in the design of a hospital?

The list of questions grew longer and quickly propelled our design team into a new mode of operation, "Safe by Design." We realized that if we wanted to significantly affect medical outcomes through the elimination of medical error in the design of a hospital, we would need to examine the design process and be willing to depart from the traditional approach.

This chapter introduces a new architectural design process called "Safe by Design," showing how it differs from the traditional design process, and how the actual culture of an architect's design studio must change if the profession is serious about providing health care environments that compel the delivery of safe, error-free care.

A Traditional Approach to Design

The Kick-Off

An architect's commission traditionally begins with a review of an owner-provided functional space program (*see* Figure 6-1, page 71), a department-by-department, room-by-room list of spaces to be incorporated into the hospital's design. The owner might have hired a health care planner to develop the program as a way of defining the scope of the project, which assists in evaluating the financial viability of the proposed facility. The program is developed in different formats and includes a variety of approaches to defining the operational or functional aspect of a proposed facility. In most cases the program gives a very limited amount of information regarding the proposed facility's function. Although a review of failure mode and effects analysis (FMEA) results from the new design process, it is estimated that approximately 70% of the active failures identified in design are attributed to operational processes and approximately 30% to latent conditions in the environment. If this is true, then why do people spend so little effort designing the operational processes *before* they design the environment that will house them? Figure 6-1 provides an example of a form used for space allocation, in this case a surgical suite. There is space for describing the rooms necessary for that function, the quantity of those rooms, and the square footage for each room.

The standard form of agreement between an owner and an architect is the American Institute of Architects' (AIA's) document B141, which is a contract used within the United States for architectural design services. It is the architect's responsibility to review the program to understand the owner's requirements. Often the owner-furnished program is accompanied by a preliminary construction budget and project schedule. These documents, the program, the construction budget, and the project schedule comprise the traditional starting point for the architect's design team to begin work.

The Schematic Design Process

With the program in hand, the architect begins to lay out the building. Doing his or her best to meet the requirements of the program, the architect begins by laying out the departments in what is often referred to as a "blocking and stacking diagram." This approach allows the architect and the facility's owner the opportunity to review the design in multiple stages or phases of development. Before the plan displays each space identified in the program, everyone involved can evaluate and agree upon the building's general configuration.

Following approval of the blocking and stacking diagram, the architect in-fills each block with the individual rooms identified in the program, thereby creating the *schematic plan*. Typically, the blocks cannot accommodate the individual rooms and must begin to evolve and develop different shapes.

The schematic plan does not include all the detail associated with the space. It often includes the layouts of walls and doors only. The AIA B141 agreement provides schematic design documents consisting of drawings and other documents that illustrate the scale and relationship of project components. This traditional approach can delay design decisions, eventually resulting in a compromise in quality

Space Allocation Profile Summary | Operating Rooms & Support

Program dated: 2/28/2005

Key Planning Unit	Qty	Sq Ft Guidelines	Notes/Comments
Management/Administrative			
• Office - Director	1	108	
• Control Center - Schedule Viewing	1	140	
• Office - Materials Coordinator	1	108	
• Pneumatic Tube Station	1	10	
		(366)	
Sterile Core & Operating Rooms			
• General Operating Room	4	600 each	
• Specialty Operating Room	4	600 each	
• Equip Support between 2 rooms	2	250 each	
• Sterile Core Per OR	8	100 each	Med Pyxis in Sterile Core
• Scrub Station	8	20 each	
• Portable X-Ray Storage	1	25	
• C-Arm Storage	1	30	
• Monitor Cart Storage	1	30	
		(6,345)	
OR General Support			
• Patient Stretcher Receiving/Staging	1	250	
• Clean Cart Delivery Area & Lift	1	125	
• Soiled Cart Return Area & Lift	1	125	
• Equipment Storage - general	1	400	
• Pathology Office & Frozen Section	1	180	
• Janitor's Closet	1	35	
• Sub-sterile Storage/Cart Staging	8	60 each	Staging/Temporary Storage along outer Circulation Corridor
• Oversized Elevator Lobby	1	300	
		(1,895)	
Staff Support			
• Locker - Male	1	200	40 people/MD & staff shared
• Shower - Male	2	20 each	
• Locker - Female	1	350	70 people/MD & staff shared
• Shower - Female	2	20 each	
• Lounge - Shared Male & Female	1	400	
		(1,030)	

Figure 6-1. Space Allocation Program.
This is an example of a Functional Space Allocation Program (or simply, the program) provided to the author to initiate the design process. Notice the room-by-room quantity and square footage listing, as well as the absence of functional or operational information in the "Notes/Comments" column. The lack of detailed operational information fails to equip the design team with the information necessary to create a health care facility that is safe by design.

Source: Gresham, Smith and Partners. Nashville, TN. Used with permission.

or added cost to the owner or architect for design changes necessary to accommodate the specific requirements of each room.

The Design Development Phase

Following the owner's approval of the schematic design documents, the architect begins to add detail to the design. With each successive phase of development a uniform level of detail, cabinetry, lighting, medical gasses, plumbing fixtures, electronic documentation system, fixed medical equipment, and so on are determined. As detail is determined, it may be necessary to revise the schematic plan decisions because the additional information can identify flaws in the schematic design. The owner and the architect must then decide whether to revise the approved schematic at an additional cost to the owner or the architect, or to compromise on the quality of the design.

Much of the functional detail is determined during this phase. The components of information technology systems, locations, and quantities of medical gas outlets, switches and controls, automation systems for medications and supplies, and so on, are drawn into the schematic plan, transforming it into the design development plan.

Occasionally, at the end of the design development phase, a mock-up of the patient rooms proposed in the design will be built. Traditionally at this stage in development, there is enough detail regarding the patient room to allow a life-size sample to be built. Hospital staff should be given time to evaluate the sample to identify any changes to make in the design. Oftentimes the evaluation is limited to the device locations within the room because a change in room size or configuration would take added time and cost for design.

The Construction Document Phase

Following the approval of the design development documents, the owner releases the architect to prepare final drawings and specification for constructing the project. These construction documents provide the contractors, subcontractors, reviewing authorities, and others with the information needed to bid and build the project.

Little interaction between the owner and the design team occurs during this phase. Architects and engineers complete the documents based on information provided to them in the preceding phases of work.

Bidding or Negotiating Phase and Construction Phase: Administration of the Construction Contract

Having completed the design, the architect helps the owner and/or the owner's contractor obtain bids for construction and offers observation during the construction phase to inform the owner of the contractor's compliance and noncompliance with the contract documents. These steps traditionally have been followed by architects in designing hospitals.

The New "Safe by Design" Approach

A departure from the traditional approach to hospital design will take us along a road not traveled before, called "Safe by Design." The remainder of the chapter will go through the steps involved in the new "Safe by Design" approach.

Phase One: The Predesign Phase

Typically the architect's commission begins with the traditional delivery of a functional space allocation program, a preliminary construction budget, and a project schedule. After a general review of these documents, the architect should begin the design process with the detailed development of the hospital operation plan. Before accepting the space allocation program, the architect should first reach a thorough understanding and agreement on *safe* operational processes that will function in the new facility.

The design process will use a team approach, bringing all the hospital operating units together. It is important to create departmental operation narratives that document how the caregivers will deliver safe care. For example, consider the medication dispensing process. Medication errors represent as much as 50% of medical errors occurring in the acute care hospital setting. Organizations make many decisions in determining the safest process for medication administration. These decisions can include using the following types of technology or processes:

- Robotic picking systems
- Electronic medication administration records
- Bar-coding systems
- Automated dispensing systems
- Pneumatic tubes
- Involving family members in medication administration

Many of the decisions affect space allocation and the project budget. Focusing on process design will allow the architect to design space that will accommodate the technology, staff, family members, equipment, and process designed by the team.

Operational process plans can take a variety of forms. If a narrative format is most acceptable and understandable by the design team, then Figure 6-2 on page 74, a sample operational narrative, would be an appropriate format. An operational narrative documents the way things will work in the proposed design. For each clinical department, the process is described, using a form such as Figure 6-2, a "clinical department profile" referring to the movement of patients in the emergency department.

Others are more comfortable with graphic representations of operational processes and so may prefer "process maps" (*see* Figure 6-3 on page 75) to document the design. This figure is a process map of a surgical suite. A process map is a pictorial description of a process, in which a circle represents beginnings or ends, rectangular shapes represent steps, and diamond shapes represent decision points.

This new design process is an excellent methodology for decision making. As the process is designed, the team should simultaneously design—to a construction document level of detail—the highly repetitive rooms that occur in the facility, such as patient rooms, exam rooms, and operating rooms. It is in these patient care areas where the interface between caregiver and patient most frequently occurs. And it is at this interface between patient and caregiver where error occurs.

Clinical Department Profile **Name** Emergency Department (...

Date Last Revised: Project #:

First Floor (Clinical)

Department Contact: Project Phase:

Email Project Manager:

Phone Phone

Client Liaison:

Client Liaison:

Process Assumptions

Process Assumption	Description/Details	Approved
Patient Access	Walk-in patients will enter the hospital through the Emergency Department Walk-In entrance. Once the patient is inside the emergency room, a greeter will meet the patient and seek to understand the reason for their visit. Triage is immediately available and has visibility over the emergency department and the greeter station. Once the greeter has determined the reason for their visit the patient will be taken back to an exam room. The patient will not stop at triage unless all of the exam rooms are occupied. Once the patient is in the exam room he/she will be triaged by a nurse. Vital signs will then be taken and the appropriate care will be given. If all of the exam rooms are occupied the patient will be taken to one of the two private triage rooms. Here they will receive a brief assessment and a quick registration will be conducted. Patients entering through the walk-in entrance that are in need of immediate emergency care, will be taken back to the appropriate room according to their level of acuity. Family members that arrive with the patient can wait in the emergency department waiting room, and a limited number can accompany the patient back to the exam room. This number will be established by hospital policy. Family members that wish to use the vending services or visit the coffee shop in the hospital lobby, will be given an in house J-tech pager. This will allow the family member to have freedom within the hospital and still be available to the doctor and the patient. Ambulance patients will be brought through the three bay ambulance garage. Based on their acuity they will be placed in a trauma room or a patient exam room. There are no fast track or minor acuity style areas within the ER. It is assumed that patients will be zoned as determined by	☐ Initial
Primary Process		

Figure 6-2. Operational Narrative.
This is an example of a narrative format description of the operational process, a clinical department profile for patients entering the emergency department. It shows the type of operational process information developed at the predesign phase of a project. The clinical department profile is maintained and updated throughout the design process. It has been described by some as an "Owner's Manual" that describes how a facility should operate after it is assembled.

Source: Gresham, Smith and Partners. Nashville, TN. Used with permission.

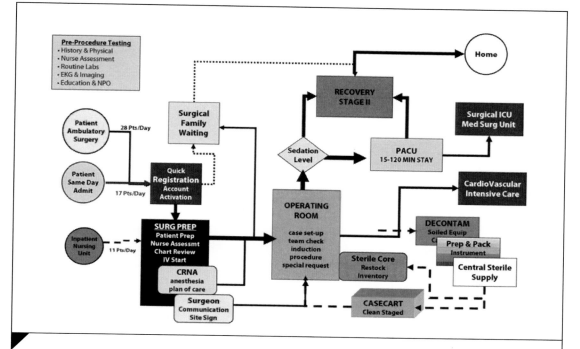

Figure 6-3. Process Map.
This is an example of a graphic representation of the operational process (a process map) for inpatients, outpatients, and emergent patients going through surgery. Developed in the predesign phase, this process map can be quickly understood at a glance and is sometimes preferred over the narrative format shown in Figure 6-2. Ideally, a combination of graphic and narrative forms is used to accurately document the operational processes designed by the team.

Source: Gresham, Smith and Partners. Nashville, TN. Used with permission.

A focus on the detailed design of the highly repetitive rooms is also mandatory to incorporate the principle of standardization in design. True standardization is the identical replication of space, and true standardization of the repetitive spaces will compel safe care and reduce error. The benefits of standardization have been realized in other industries for years and must be incorporated into health care designs. Standardization provides environmental familiarity for the hospital staff, which in turn allows the efficient use of time and space, reduces stress and fatigue (which are often root causes of error), and reduces the facility's construction and operating costs.

Figure 6-4 (page 76) is an example of a standardized patient room safe-by-design. The floor plan drawing shown is accompanied by interior elevation drawings, reflected ceiling plans, and other documents that denote the standardized locations of medical gases, switches, medical equipment, light fixtures, mechanical diffusers, and all other devices provided by the design. A focus on detail in the predesign phase equips the architect with an accurate footprint of the repetitive rooms and makes true standardization possible in the subsequent phases of design.

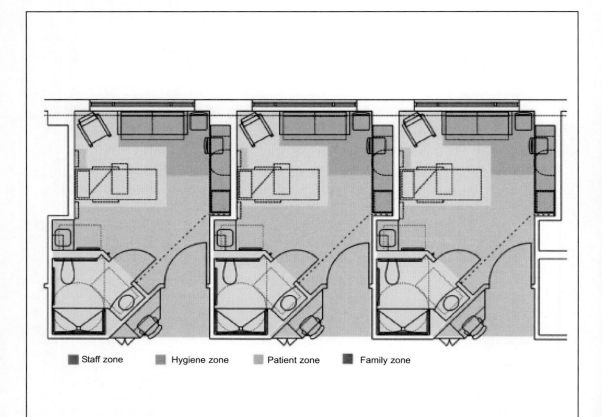

Figure 6-4. Standardized Patient Room.
This is an example of a standardized patient room that was developed early in the pre-design phase, and was then developed into a detailed drawing used for construction of a full site mock-up room in the concept design phase.

Source: Gresham, Smith and Partners. Nashville, TN. Used with permission.

A focus on process design and a detailed design of the highly repetitive rooms requires the involvement of other design team members who traditionally would not be significantly active until the project's design development phase. For example, the electrical engineer may be involved with the design and placement of normal and emergency power outlets, lighting fixtures and controls, and coordination of the low-voltage systems such as nurse call, code blue, paging, and phone systems. The engineer might also coordinate and work with medical equipment designers of physiological monitoring systems, telemetry systems, or other similar technologies.

The mechanical engineer may provide heating, ventilating, and air-conditioning system requirements and will locate the diffusers and grilles for supply, return, and exhausted air. Air quality requirements that affect air movement and filtration will be established. The temperature and humidity control device location will be determined at this stage.

The plumbing designer may specify the types of hand-washing sinks, toilet and shower fixtures, hands-free controls, and fire-suppression sprinkler head types and locations.

The medical equipment planner may determine the design of physiological monitoring systems, patient bed types and features, headwall units, exam lights, and other equipment specified and provided by the owner.

The information technology designer may specify the type and locations for electronic medical records or bar-coding systems.

Other design team members may include special lighting designers, acoustical engineers, or graphic designers. All these design team members fulfill an important role and bring their expertise to bear on the project in the predesign phase.

Therefore, focusing efforts on the design of process and the highly repetitive rooms during the predesign phase will eliminate compromises in safety and quality, as the design takes shape in the subsequent phases of development.

Phase Two: The Concept Design Phase

Equipped with an operations plan and a detailed design of the repetitive rooms, the architect is able to amend the original space program and develop a conceptual design. The conceptual design will evolve from bubble diagrams to block diagrams and will delineate the scale and relationships between the different operating units within the facility. Stairs, elevators, and visitor, staff, and service entrances will be positioned. The development of the conceptual design is not significantly different from the traditional approach to design except that the concept design is based on a more detailed and accurate knowledge of the project and how the concept design is used to prepare for the schematic design phase. The following three figures demonstrate the development of the conceptual design, showing how a conceptual bubble diagram (as shown in Figure 6-5 on page 78) evolves through an intermediary step (as shown in Figure 6-6 on page 79) into a conceptual block diagram (as shown in Figure 6-7 on page 80). A conceptual bubble diagram is a general pictorial description of adjacencies of services and departments. It shows the relationships between services and provides a general idea of which services should be near each other.

Next, Figure 6-6 on page 79 combines a conceptual bubble diagram with a block diagram to illustrate the general adjacencies with some more explicit relationships. The combination provides a more definitive description of the relationship between services.

Finally, Figure 6-7 on page 80, a conceptual block diagram, is the most explicit of the three diagrams, showing exact physical relationships between services and departments.

Two significant opportunities exist at this stage of the design to improve the quality and safety of the project. First, FMEA is used to evaluate the conceptual design and identify potential failure modes or errors. At this stage of the design, the departmental adjacencies are evaluated, focusing on the flow of a patient through the system from admission to discharge. Several templates exist that can be used for

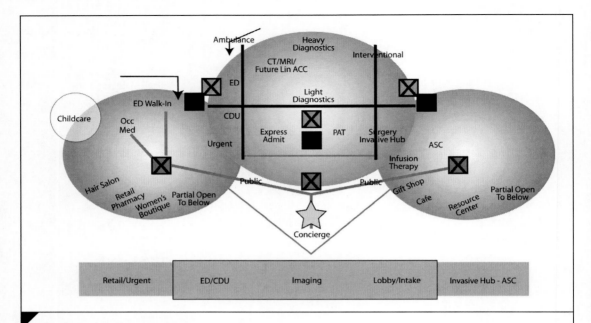

Figure 6-5. Conceptual Bubble Diagram.
This is an example of a bubble diagram at the initiation of the concept design phase.
This diagram positions the operational units present on the main level of the facility.
Vertical and horizontal circulation routes of patients, staff, and visitors are delineated.
Shown are the size and the location of the facility's major elements that support the flow
of the patient, staff, visitors, and supplies that are required by the operational plan.
Similar diagrams are prepared for each level of the proposed facility, which delineate the
vertical relationships between the major elements of the facility.

Source: Gresham, Smith and Partners. Nashville, TN. Used with permission.

an FMEA in a health care setting. However, many are too complex and time consuming for most applications. The following template for FMEA analysis (shown in Figure 6-8 on page 81) might prove to be useful.

Figure 6-8 is an example of an FMEA performed at the conceptual design phase of a project. During this phase we test the safety of patient flows between the different operating units shown in the concept plan. Subsequent analyses performed at the later phase of development use the same FMEA format; however, different aspects of the design are tested.

In this format the first column, "Potential Failure/Effect Mode," identifies all the possible failures that could occur during the identified scenario.

The second column, "Frequency of Occurrence," rates the frequency of the event, with a score of Low (1), occurring once a year; Med (2), occurring once a month; and High (3), occurring once a week. The same is true with the "Severity of Effect" column, which rates the severity of the event with scores

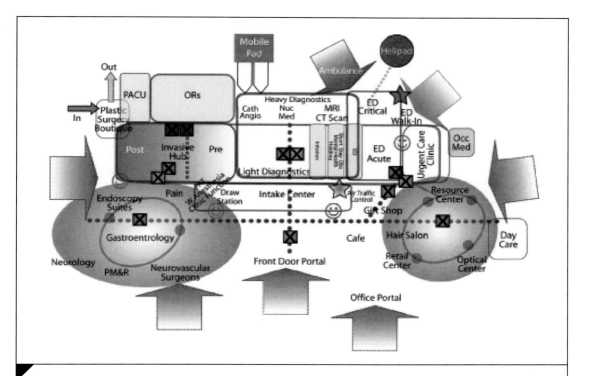

Figure 6-6. Conceptual Bubble/Block Diagram.
This example of a bubble/block diagram demonstrates how the bubble diagram begins to evolve into a conceptual floor plan. The various operational functions occurring on the main level are further defined in size and shape. Additional information is shown that precisely supports the operational plan for the facility.

Source: Gresham, Smith and Partners. Nashville, TN. Used with permission.

of Low (2), patient dissatisfaction; Med (4), patient is harmed; and High (6), patient death.

The fourth column, "Guiding Principles," is another evaluation that is unrelated to safety or harm that may elevate an effect to a higher priority.

The "Priority Score" column is the numeric value established for each event.

Frequency + Severity = (Range 3 to 9) Rankings lower than 6 require a plan for correction. All rankings of 6 or higher require correction.

In the column, "Required Change," the architect determines if the change is related to process or to the physical environment. The architect then identifies possible changes to mitigate the effect of the event in the "Possible Changes" column. Following this, the architect determines if the cost is operational or a one-time capital expense, and the amount, if possible. The architect will then give a recommendation. It is important to note that all errors are unacceptable; however, the situation may require

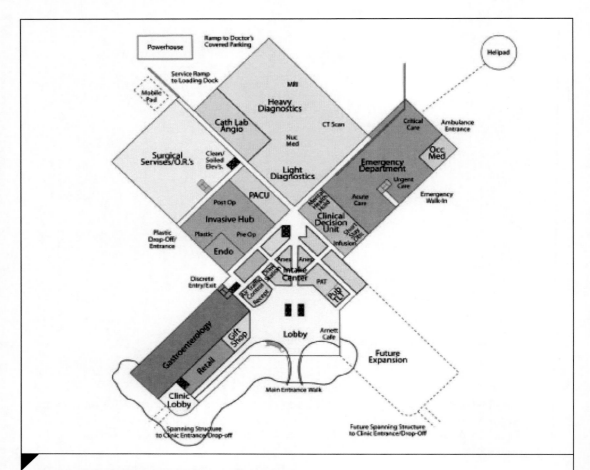

Figure 6-7. Conceptual Block Diagram.
This is a typical conceptual block diagram of the facility main level. Similar diagrams are prepared for each level of the facility and together constitute the conceptual plan. The locations, size, and general shape of each operating unit within the facility are shown. Major vertical and horizontal circulation routes are clearly delineated. Future expansion zones are also shown.

Source: Gresham, Smith and Partners. Nashville, TN. Used with permission.

some corrections to be scheduled for future incorporation into the facility plan.

Identifying failures in a design and/or a process at this stage of a project allows correction without a loss of time or any additional cost. The concept is quickly and easily modified and captures the opportunity for improvement.

In addition, it is important to evaluate the design of the repetitive rooms by building life-size samples called mock-ups, which allow simulation and testing for potential failures or even quality improve-

Potential Failure/Effect Mode	Frequency of Occurrence	Severity of Effect	Guiding Principles	Priority Score	Required Change	Possible Change(s)	Probable Cost	Recommendation
	l/m/h	l/m/h	l/m/h	(3-9)	(Process/Design)			
Misses her bus	low	med	low	5	Design	* OB ambulance entry to receive Mom & Baby	* No additional cost	* Discreet entrance into OB Screen already incorporated in current design
Can't get taxi	low	med	low	5	Design	* OB ambulance entry to receive Mom & Baby	* No additional cost	* Discreet entrance into OB Screen already incorporated in current design
Goes thru wrong door	high	med	high	7	Design Process/Design	* Clear identification of appropriate entry * Provide facilitated entry w/personal curbside mobility assistance in reaching destination	* No additional cost * Operational cost	* Incorporated into current design * Recommend incorporating this concept or appropriate alternate into current design
Can't find parking space	med	low	high	4	Process/Design	* Valet Parking	* Operational cost	* Continue to evaluate during design development
May go to women's care clinic	med	low	low	4	Process/Design	* Re-direct and provide assistance to destination	* No additional cost	* Clear, concise signage to support simplified wayfinding in current design
Could go to the walk-in clinic	med	med	med	6	Process	* Re-direct and provide assistance to destination	* Operational cost	* Recommend establishing process/protocol based on patient condition
Could go to wrong clinic	low	med	med	5	Process	* Re-direct and provide assistance to destination	* Operational cost	* Recommend establishing process/protocol based on patient condition
Could go to wrong building	high	med	high	7	Design	* Clear identification of appropriate entry	* Operational cost	* Clear, concise signage to support simplified wayfinding in current design & establishing protocol for assistnace based on patient condition

Figure 6-8. FMEA Sample Form.
This example relates to a woman in labor heading to the hospital and finding the labor and delivery department. In this template, each potential failure is identified, and the effect of that failure is judged by frequency, severity, and guiding principle. The priority score is the importance of all those factors added. The form provides space for listing the changes along with their probable cost, and for listing final recommendations.

Source: Gresham, Smith and Partners. Nashville, TN. Used with permission.

ment. Because of their background and training, architects can often visualize space in three dimensions while viewing two-dimensional drawings; most other people cannot. A mock-up gives users the opportunity to simulate and test the room in its actual size and configuration, provides the ideal setting to test and evaluate different equipment options, and acts as a training and orientation room that prepares users to safely transition into the new facility.

Taking time within the conceptual design phase to evaluate, simulate, test, and confirm the operational plan and the concept design is a major departure from the traditional approach. A well-defined conceptual design will assure the successful and timely execution of a schematic design and will avoid the design compromises that often result in latent conditions that support active failures.

Phase Three: The Schematic Design Phase
The architect now has a complete understanding of how the new facility will operate. The conceptual plan and the repetitive rooms have been designed, tested, revised, and finalized. The space required to support the operations and safe functioning of the repetitive rooms is well understood and the architect is now ready to lay out the schematic plan.

The schematic plan is the space-by-space, room-by-room layout of the facility. This phase of development, which traditionally requires multiple attempts and design adjustments and redesign after redesign, is accomplished accurately in the first schematic plan. Architects are trained to design space that reflects their understanding of the clients' needs. Providing the architect with a complete and accurate understanding of the project through detailed operational narrative, space allocation, and redundant room design assures the successful development of the schematic plan.

In hospital design, a major portion of the facility is redundant space, such as patient rooms, exam rooms, and surgical suites. Having a major portion of the facility designed to the construction document level of detail provides a much more accurate schematic plan. These major portions of the building can now be budgeted with established costs rather than estimated costs. The actual cost of the building can be derived from the use of mock-ups and the construction document level of detail for the redundant rooms—a significant advantage of the new design process.

The new process also offers a significant time saving. The work accomplished in the predesign and concept phases of the project allows the schematic design to be developed accurately in one or two weeks, as opposed to months of time used inefficiently producing multiple schemes that reflect only partial success. It may seem that the time spent in the predesign and concept design phases of the project would increase the total design time for a project. However, the time is quickly redeemed in the schematic design, design development, and construction document phases of the project. The overall design schedule duration is the same for projects that would traditionally fall in the 9- to 12-month range. For larger projects whose design duration would traditionally exceed 12 months, significant time savings could be achieved, because the proportion of redundant (standardized) space increases.

Therefore, reordering the decision-making process by focusing on the facility operation and redundant room design eliminates time-consuming and costly redesigns characteristic of the traditional trial-and-error approach to design. Thus, a client's need for a healing environment that compels the delivery of safe, error-free care is quickly met in the development of the schematic plan "Safe by Design."

Phase Four: The Design Development Phase

The design development phase of the project in the "safe by design" approach is much less time consuming when compared to the traditional approach to design. Because the repetitive rooms have been designed to the construction document level of detail, a major portion of the facility has been completely developed. The architect now focuses the client on the remaining unique space within the building.

Understanding the facility operations allows the design team to determine the detail design of the unique spaces quickly and accurately. The remaining details, such as cabinetry, lighting, medical gases, and plumbing fixtures, are delineated in appropriate forms and included in the design development package. Because much of the detail has been determined in the previous phases, the design development phase is much shorter in duration and less complex.

It is during this phase of the process that the vendors for dietary, radiology, and other medical equipment prepare their detailed site-specific designs. The vendor drawings become part of the design development package and provide vital information to the architects and engineers, which will allow a quick and accurate completion of the design in the construction document phase of the project.

Often the construction cost will be established based on the design development documents. Using a process-led design approach assures the owner and the architect that unexpected changes in the construction cost will be avoided because the project scope is clearly understood and developed.

Phase Five: The Construction Document Phase

The approved design development documents establish a firm foundation for the construction document phase. In this phase, the architects and engineers focus on the preparation of thorough drawings and specifications that will be issued for bidding and construction of the project.

Very little collaboration between the owner and the design team occurs at this stage. The architects and engineers have been equipped with a detailed and accurate understanding of the client's needs, and now they can focus on completing the drawings and coordination of each discipline's work. The construction documents consist of drawings and specifications that direct the contractor, subcontractors, reviewing authorities, and others involved in the construction of the project.

The latter phases of the design process, such as the construction document phase, bidding and negotiating phase, and the construction administration phase, do not significantly differ from the traditional approach.

Phase Six: The Bidding and Negotiating Phase

The architect helps the owner get qualified bids or negotiates bids for the construction of the project. This phase is similar to the traditional approach except that the architect must meet with the bidders in a pre-bid conference to inform them of the safety-driven design principles used in the development of the project. Many contractors and subcontractors in the health care market are unfamiliar with principles such as true standardization and should be informed of the financial and time savings attributes associated with these principles. It is the zero-tolerance approach with true standardization that differentiates a traditional hospital design from one that is "Safe by Design."

Phase Seven: The Construction Administration

During construction, the architect maintains his or her involvement by periodically observing the construction and advises the owner of compliance or lack of compliance with the construction documents' intent.

Conclusion

As a licensed architect, each time I place my signature and seal on a document for the construction of a hospital, I have committed to protect the health, safety, and welfare of the employees, visitors, patients, and others who enter the building. Awareness of the impact that the physical environment has on the delivery of safe, error-free health care has changed my entire perspective on my profession.

Designing safe space for the provision of error-free care demands a departure from the traditional approach to health care facility design. The safe-by-design approach described in this chapter enables the health care planning and design community to produce designs that compel the delivery of safe care.

Initially, the safe-by-design approach shifts much of the design detail to the earliest possible time in the process. Furthermore, it employs time-tested principles from other industries, such as standardization and FMEA analysis. Its focus is on the development of process design, which is then supported by facility design. The new approach offers caregivers the opportunity to simulate and test the design in life-size physical mock-ups while there is time to improve the design. It may also reduce design duration by replacing the trial and error, design, and redesign approach with a knowledge-based design approach. In addition, it may reduce the cost and duration of construction by standardization of the redundant spaces and process within the facility. It *will* result in a facility design that minimizes latent conditions that promote medical error; and it *will* result in the highest-quality, safest hospital design possible for management, staff, and patients.

Chapter 7

Fostering Medical Staff Involvement in Facility Design and Safety Culture

by John W. Overton Jr., M.D.

"We are causing harm. We need to stop." (Donald Berwick, M.D., keynote address presented at the 11th National Forum on Quality Improvement in Healthcare. Institute for Healthcare Improvement, New Orleans, Dec. 7, 1999.)

Physician involvement in health care facility design creates numerous opportunities for improving safety and efficiency and provides refreshing impetus for initiatives in health care safety. Yet engaging medical staff in the evolution of safety culture and facility design can present daunting challenges. Safety science in commercial aviation and nuclear power plant operation has been rigorously studied over the past two decades; however, in health care a dedicated focus on error, adverse events, and patient injury has occurred only in the past six to eight years. So, relative to aviation, the science and tools used in health care are young. This book, in fact, is one of the earliest additions of its kind to the field of safety science. The two goals of this chapter are to address the tumultuous terrain of recruiting physician support for a culture of safety, and to involve medical staff in hospital design in which the design model is centered on maximizing safety in patient care. The challenges presented by these issues are complex, however, and can only be introduced, but in no way solved, in a short chapter. The hope is to give stakeholders who are involved in health care delivery questions that generate reflective inquiry, discussion, redirection, and—ultimately—improvements in safety.

The author, a cardiac surgeon, has had 15 years of cardiothoracic surgical experience that followed 6 years in the practice of emergency medicine. Other career-long interests are trauma, EMS systems, and critical care; he is a diplomat of the American Boards of Thoracic Surgery, General Surgery, and Emergency Medicine. He served as a Team Leader for 1 of 44 hospitals in the Institute for Healthcare Improvement's (IHI's) Breakthrough Series on Improving Outcomes in Adult Cardiac Surgery in the late 1990s. In addition, he has been a general aviation pilot since 1977 and remains active as a pilot today. For many years he has been interested in safety issues in health care and in aviation, and since prostate cancer forced him to stop practicing surgery in 2000, he has had more time to devote to safety issues. Since 2001 he has communicated with and learned from Professor Robert Helmreich, University of Texas, the father of crew resource management, and from other colleagues at the University of Texas in the field of safety in aviation and other high-risk industries. Currently, he serves on the Board of Directors of the Commission on Accreditation of Medical Transport Systems, the only body in the United States that accredits aeromedical transportation systems.

Before discussing the culture of safety, two concepts require brief clarification. The term *medical staff* used in this chapter refers specifically to physicians. The discussion of *health care safety* refers not only to the safety of patients but also the safety of those who provide patient care. This includes physicians, nurses, therapists, pharmacists, administrators, medical transport teams, and other staff who support the care process. Certainly all providers of patient care are vulnerable to hazards and errors, as are our patients.

The Need for Physician Involvement in Safe Design

The concept of medical staff involvement in hospital facility design is exciting. As our organizations strive to learn, we should seek input about facility design from those physicians who work at the point of care—the "sharp end" of care delivery. The involvement of medical staff in design is a novel yet potentially productive component to traditional hospital facility design.

Several articles have been written about physician involvement with multidisciplinary teams in the design of critical care units in the 1980s[1] and 1990s[2,3]; an occasional reference to medical staff involvement in facility design appeared in earlier decades.[4] Over the past several years, physicians have taken more active roles in facility design based on safety concepts.[5–7] The evolution of intensive care unit design over the past decade has also recently been reviewed, noting positive and negative trends in design and function.[8] Although some safety experts argue that we have made real progress in patient safety, considerable evidence suggests that since the Institute of Medicine's (IOM's) report *To Err Is Human* was published, we have made some, although little, progress in health care safety.[9] At best our progress has been only modest.[10,11]

On January 17, 2007, the Minnesota Department of Health issued its third annual public report on preventable adverse health events in Minnesota, showing increases in adverse events and a doubling of preventable patient deaths in Minnesota hospitals from October 2005 to October 2006, when compared with the prior reporting year.[12] It appears that the reporting system is functioning as intended, and this is a positive observation. Whether some portion of the reported increase in adverse events is secondary to better reporting is unclear; nevertheless, the apparent increase in adverse events and deaths is most alarming. Hopefully the reports on adverse events will provide insight into why such events occur, and help to modify systems for safety improvement and promote countermeasures that will eliminate these preventable events. Are we failing to reduce errors and losing ground in efforts to improve health care safety?

If few medical staff support safety culture and safety change concepts, the adverse events and injury will continue to proliferate. Without collaboration between strong medical staff leadership and other leaders in health care, the evolution of safety culture and safer facility design in health care is doubtful. Physician involvement with other health care leaders is essential for achieving new goals for safety. However, creation of a safety culture cannot be forced. Learning and change cannot be unwillingly imposed on physicians or any group. But how do we encourage physicians to join the move toward a new culture of safety?

Medical Staff Commonality and Heterogeneity

Most health care providers are independent and autonomous, pride themselves in their autonomy, and often attribute portions of their academic or career successes to this autonomy. Although physician independence and autonomy could partially explain why many physicians have excellent diagnostic skills, these attributes may not be as positive when physicians need to function on teams, speak with a common voice, or move together to lead or embrace cultural change.

Physicians do share some other *commonalities,* in addition to valuing autonomy. They care deeply about the well-being of their patients and want the best attainable outcomes for them. Most physicians feel gratitude for excellent educations and the opportunity to serve those who are ill, injured, stressed, and often frightened and in pain. What opportunities their medical careers have provided have given them the ability to provide this service.

Physicians also share a deep sense of authority and responsibility and have been educated to believe that adverse events and patient injuries occur because of mistakes made at the point of care. Surgeons and others who provide procedural care believe that their outcomes are due primarily to their technical skills, speed, efficiency, and individual ability. Historically, little of their training has involved teamwork, team leadership, learning about improving communications, and the impact of human factors training. Physicians have had little or no training in risk management or threat and error management.

Although physicians share some commonalities, to a larger extent they comprise a *heterogeneous* lot. The evolution of health care and their education as professionals has been fragmented. Traditionally, they have received their education and training in "silos," or by discipline. Rarely, if ever, do medical students learn or train with nurses, pharmacists, or therapists, not to mention those in health care administration or public health.

Although most physicians share a desire to serve mankind, their personal motivations, interests, goals, and practice philosophies differ. Even within specialty and subspecialty groups of physicians, considerable differences exist in individual goals and motivation. Within specialty groups, a wide variation in physician "career anchors" has been found[13] and may, in part, explain suboptimal communications, problems with hand offs in care, and differences in philosophy about patient care within professional groups.

In the contemporary practice environment, many members of the medical staff are driven to provide more care and services with fewer resources of time, staff, and money. Annual income for many physicians has fallen dramatically over the past decade, introducing considerable personal and family stress, as well as lifestyle changes. Some physicians have sought alternative sources of income that might not be directly related to the care they provide for patients. An example of this is purchasing ownership in freestanding procedural facilities (surgery centers, radiology centers, and cardiac catheterization labs) or specialty hospitals (cardiac surgical centers of excellence and others). Some of these facilities have provided outstanding and efficient patient care, although numerous issues, conflicts, and challenges have also resulted from these innovative financial solutions.

Many physicians are severely, chronically fatigued, chronically stressed, and have remarkably limited resilience. Their abilities and reserves to "run faster" and "do more" have been reached and sustained over a number of years. They are "maxed out" in many ways. As a result, empathy for patients may be suboptimal, and less time is spent listening to patients and colleagues. In other words, physicians barely cope with "fixing the broken part," and rarely have the time or stamina to serve as the caring listeners, advisors, or mentors that most patients seek.[14] Physicians may also have little discretionary time for, and often little interest in, obtaining new education, training, or skills. They need a break: How can they sustain and revitalize themselves?

These factors can lead health care providers to become irritable and isolated, less interested and less involved in hospital and other organizational issues, and even angry. A colleague recently communicated that he believes many physicians today "feel like caged animals—they are angry and feel under constant attack by patients, patient families, colleagues, administrators, attorneys, insurers, legislators and occasionally by even their own families, who never get to see them."[15]

Understanding Physicians' Resistance to Safety Culture

Today the health care field is facing problems with access to care, the costs of care, and dealing with the uninsured. Many in health care believe that the delivery system is failing and unsustainable. Although physicians are slowly embracing the need for improvement in health care safety, major challenges exist relative to legislative support for health care solutions, the power of lobbying groups, a lack of a common voice from physicians, issues with insurers, third-party payers, the pharmaceutical industry, and elimination of corruption. Because improving the culture of safety and designing facilities to promote safe care are vitally important, numerous other challenges must be addressed to provide the hope for the future that physicians and patients need, and to ensure the survival of quality and affordable care. It is likely that physician support for safety culture initiatives will be lukewarm at best without concomitant progress on these other challenging fronts.

Several significant obstacles to medical staff support and wholehearted endorsement of safety culture exist. First, the most obvious triad that needs to be addressed is the following:

1. To believe a problem exists with health care safety
2. To believe that practical and cost-effective solutions with proven outcomes to improve safety exist
3. To believe that the medical community shares general beliefs and values about the importance of addressing safety in health care

In addition, concerns about widespread failure of practice and business models in health care and other industries over the past one to two decades, and concerns about the risk of medical malpractice litigation, provide additional obstacles in the journey toward safety culture. These points are briefly considered below.

Acknowledging the Problem with Safety in Health Care

Medical providers now read daily reports from the lay press and safety experts about deficiencies in patient safety. However, many providers have only infrequently seen or heard of an adverse event that involved patients in their own care. Many providers believe that adverse events happen to the patients of other providers, but never to their own patients, and thus believe that the problem of adverse events has been overstated. Some providers might have witnessed a preventable adverse patient event only rarely throughout their entire career. This might be the result of a tendency to observe primarily that which one feels capable of correcting individually. Only by looking at the bigger picture can providers recognize the magnitude of the problems in patient safety.

To illustrate the difficulty in acknowledging that a problem in health care safety exists, recall the Minnesota Department of Health report on adverse events referenced above. The total number of adverse events reported was 154 in 2.6 million hospital days. Thus, the likelihood of an adverse event occurring is roughly 5.6 adverse events per every 100,000 hospital days. Although the ideal is to see the number of adverse events approach zero, the number of reported events is actually quite low. This might help explain why many providers have had difficulty understanding the magnitude of the safety problem in health care.

When physicians have responded to surveys about their individual traits, they have often responded that they rarely make errors, operate as reliably when fatigued as when well rested, and perform as well in emergencies as in elective situations.[16] A generally held sense of infallibility, along with little personal experience with adverse events in their own patients, can make internalizing the reality of the problem with adverse events difficult for many providers. In addition, the fact that patients usually die individually, rather than in groups (as in aviation accidents), and die in health care facilities where one usually expects them to die, are other factors that make believing in the magnitude of the safety problem difficult for physicians to comprehend. Accepting the magnitude of the problem of adverse events has been slow not only among health care providers, but even among groups of patients.[17]

Minimal Outcome Data Supporting Safety "Fixes"

Numerous suggestions to promote safety have been offered by safety experts from other high-risk industries, as well as from health care consultants. Examples of such suggestions are additional education in team training, improved communication skills, better understanding of human factors, direct observation of procedures, and simulated medical and surgical scenarios. Although many of these recommendations to promote health care safety have strong intuitive or face validity, data about the outcomes and cost effectiveness of such innovations are just beginning to be studied. Some of the innovations that have been studied have produced mixed results. For example, outcome data supporting the benefits of using "rapid response teams" in hospitals have raised questions about the effectiveness of such teams.[18]

Other areas of controversy exist. Agreeing on definitions, including what constitutes a medical error, and selecting appropriate metrics to use for determining valid rates are ongoing challenges that have recently been reviewed by Pronovost, Miller, and Wachter.[19] The correlation between recommended process measures and positive outcome measures might not always exist.[20] Although there is increasing evidence that structural measures (how health care is organized) are important in patient safety, the science linking structure to patient safety outcomes is just beginning.

Regarding safety measurement, various tools have been developed to assess safety culture, such as the Agency for Healthcare Research and Quality (AHRQ) Hospital Survey on Patient Safety Culture[21] and a survey developed by Dr. Bryan Sexton and colleagues. Sexton's survey tool has been validated and provides a useful resource that will see increasing application as organizations attempt to understand their members' commitment to safety.[19]

The public reporting of health outcomes and pay for performance are two methods that have been proposed to improve quality and safety in health care. A recently published preliminary review of the effectiveness of pay for performance in the Centers for Medicare & Medicaid Services (CMS) Premier Hospital Quality Incentive Demonstration revealed that financial incentives conferred an adjusted incremental effect of only 2.6% to 4.1%.[22] Only time and additional data will reveal whether financial incentives will provide adequate augmented outcomes to justify the cost of these programs.

In an era of diminishing financial resources to fund new initiatives, physicians have been slow to endorse unproven strategies. Yet without new ideas and research, it will not be possible to discover new avenues to safer, higher-quality, and more efficient health care.

Heterogeneous Beliefs About Safety Culture

Although all medical providers desire safety for their patients and their staff, they hold disparate beliefs about the priorities for achieving safety. These differences exist even within specialty groups. Beliefs and values vary among physicians regarding their professional and personal lives. Even within professional practices, physicians experience considerable variability in thinking about accountability, responsibility, and balancing professional demands with personal and family needs. Obtaining general consensus on values and beliefs for patient care in general, and professional conduct even within small specialized groups, can be challenging and divisive. So far, attempts to align physician beliefs around safety culture have produced mixed results.

Given the slow rate of acknowledgment and internalization of the problem of health care safety, the paucity of outcome data to date on proposed "fixes" for safety issues, and the diversity of shared beliefs and values about patient care and safety culture, the lethargic movement of physicians toward embracing safety concepts and culture is not difficult to understand.

Other Areas of Resistance

Some of the attempts in the 1990s to consolidate hospitals and physician groups using horizontal or vertical integration have provided little, if any, benefit. For many, the consolidation of medical practice management was also a failure.[23] Cameron and Quinn have pointed out that numerous attempts at using Total Quality Management, reengineering, and downsizing to create organizational change in various industries over the past two decades have failed. The failures often occurred because cultural change did not accompany structural and process change.[24] In addition, the necessary psychological and emotional transitions of cultural change did not accompany the change process.

The area of medical malpractice litigation is another area of concern to every health care provider. Providers feel daily concern about the potential threat of malpractice litigation. Clearly, such anxiety slows any adoption of safety culture, a reporting culture, and a just culture. One possibility that could counteract this anxiety is making major improvements in fairness and equitable reward for injuries from adverse events. Such assistance may directly accompany growing support of safety culture by physicians. Would not active attempts to couple the growth of safety culture with equitable financial reward for patient injuries provide healing and fairness?

Health care has much to learn from the commercial aviation industry about nonjeopardy reporting and implementation of just culture. Total acceptance of nonjeopardy reporting and resolution of issues in the reporting environment have not completely occurred in commercial aviation, but aviation leads health care by a decade or more in the journey to safety culture.[25]

To summarize, medical providers, despite their leisurely pace to embrace safety culture, are increasingly learning of empowered, vocal patients and cost-pressured payers who are demanding accountability from health care providers, and insisting they address the alarm surrounding preventable adverse events.[26] As providers become more aware of the challenges in delivering safer health care, many have observed in their own personal experiences as patients, or from the experiences of their families, an adverse event or near miss. For all these reasons, the time has arrived for physicians to move in unison to embrace safety culture.

New Opportunities for Learning in Health Care Safety

Although the journey to safer health care is in its early stages, it is possible to be optimistic about physician support for safety initiatives and safety culture. Such support cannot be forced, but it is likely to evolve primarily out of the deep concern that physicians feel for patients and their families. No one can predict exactly where the future in health care and safety will lead. However, as Professor Edgar Schein has pointed out, change will occur frequently and more rapidly than it has before.[27] To deal with rapid change, health care providers must be willing to learn new material continuously, share the learning in our organizations, and demonstrate flexibility and resilience. Given current professional demands, developing such characteristics will prove challenging.

Many of those who are interested in health care safety believe that attempts to improve safety will have associated improvements in the quality of care and in waste reduction. This concept has strong external validity, although only time and data will provide such answers.

Physicians have been trained to heal the sick and "fix broken parts." Not only must they become more proactive about preventive medicine, but they must also become more proactive about issues relating to safety. Traditionally, the approach to "putting out fires" on the wards has been reactive. But it is important not to wait and deal only with preventable adverse events and near misses. Rather, physicians must proactively consider risks associated with all their undertakings. Proactive risk assessment is especially critical when undertaking new procedures or initiatives. Breaking the reactive mind-set and adopting a proactive stance for safety might be difficult for physicians, based on their training and experiences, but it is essential.

Recall the commercial air carriers' journey to improved safety: They realized two decades ago that they cannot await the infrequent major aviation disaster to improve safety in their daily operations. They consider evaluation of threats and errors for every flight segment and from time to time have professional observers monitor their routine operations (Line Operation Safety Audits). What might we learn and incorporate in health care from their models, to become more proactive for safety?

Traditionally in health care and many other high-risk industries, risk management and safety management have been separate functions. This is common today, even in industries much further along in the development of safety culture than health care, such as commercial aviation. Interesting new models have now integrated risk and safety management to improve effectiveness and efficiency. Such models are currently used by the Australian Defence Force, the Royal Australian Air Force, the Royal Air Force (United Kingdom), and the Canadian Defence Force. Some aero-medical transport programs in the United States, Canada, and several other nations have recently adopted and are using such an integrated model of risk and safety management. All our health care organizations, from hospitals to individual private practices, might learn from the integration of risk and safety management. Risk management is the culture, processes, and structures that are directed toward the effective management of potential opportunities and adverse events. Safety management systems provide a business-like approach to safety and are systematic, explicit, and comprehensive processes for managing safety risks.[28]

Medical staff leaders and others seriously interested in adopting changes to promote safety will need additional education in risk and safety management, communications, teamwork, and human factors because the vocabulary, concepts, and metrics in these disciplines are different from what is learned in traditional medical education. Some time will be required to learn how this additional training can be provided for busy, stressed, chronically fatigued physicians.

One important step in this process is for university undergraduate and graduate education to initiate educational programs in safety management, teamwork, communications, systems thinking, and human factors engineering. It is also vital to educate medical providers about nonjeopardy reporting, just culture, and experiences with reporting systems in other disciplines. In addition, medical students must learn principles of threat and error management and how to develop countermeasures to trap threats and errors and prevent or ameliorate adverse events. Ideally, the future will see the development of interdisciplinary education in graduate medical education, involving teamwork across all health care fields to solve problems and improve safety, quality, and effectiveness in health care. A postgraduate fellowship program in risk and safety management for health care professions could have potential and provide future leadership and resources for safety initiatives.

Medical staff and organizational leadership must judiciously allocate limited resources to recommendations for safety initiatives. Because a given tool has worked to improve safety in other fields does not guarantee success as a health care safety initiative. However, it is important to remain open-minded about learning from other disciplines. Much of what this author has learned about safety has been learned from commercial aviation. I have had the great privilege to work and study with those I consider to be the "senior deans" of commercial aviation safety, and I feel deeply indebted to these wonderful teachers and mentors. Hopefully all physicians can be open to learning from other disciplines, while keeping in mind the unique attributes and challenges of health care.

Fostering Medical Staff Collaboration in Safety Initiatives and Facility Design

Contributions by physicians in developing safety initiatives and facility design are critical to the success of those efforts. While respecting the clinical experience, judgment, and time constraints of physicians, remember that few, if any, medical staff have had education in risk or safety management, teamwork, communications, or facility design. In fact, it is likely that most physicians have never been asked

Personal Experience with the Use of Checklists in Cardiac Surgery

In the late 1990s our cardiac surgical practice of 10 surgeons noted that operative mortality was higher in one of the four hospitals in which we regularly performed cardiac operations. We had excellent data from all four institutions, which we contributed regularly to the National Cardiac Surgical Database. Neither the surgeons in our group nor an outside epidemiological consultant were able to identify the specific drivers of mortality in this one institution. Our intuition was that part of the explanation might be inadequate communications at times during hand offs in patient care; however, we could not prove that theory with our data, or with surveys or interviews with the physicians and nurses providing surgical care.

The administration at this hospital and our surgical group decided to join the Institute for Healthcare Improvement's (IHI's) Breakthrough Series in Improving Adult Cardiac Surgery. Three of the 4 hospitals in which we operated ended up participating in the IHI Collaborative and consisted of 3 of 44 organizations involved in this Collaborative for two years.

I was asked to function as the team leader for the hospital in which our mortality was higher than in our other facilities. We carefully analyzed each step in our patient care process and subsequently reengineered the structure of our care delivery model. Our efforts reduced the length of stay for elective coronary bypass surgery from 7.3 to 4.1 days, and we reduced surgical mortality from roughly 3.5% to 2.0%. Our team and hospital were pleased with the improved patient outcomes, which we sustained.

Six months after the conclusion of the IHI Breakthrough Series Collaborative, I was taking a patient off cardiopulmonary circulatory support after replacing his aortic valve. The patient was in his late 50s, and although he resumed his own native circulatory support, the patient's cardiac performance and blood pressure were not as adequate as I had predicted they would be. I elected to put the patient back on bypass for some additional support, and the second time we separated from bypass his blood pressure and cardiac output were greatly improved. We checked the valve function with ultrasound, and the movement of the valve leaflets looked normal. I learned later that on the first attempt to separate from bypass, the patient's core temperature and hemoglobin were lower than I had realized and lower than what was considered ideal. The patient had a normal recovery from surgery with no adverse outcome.

At home that evening I felt disturbed about our poor job as a team in taking that patient off bypass. This 58-year-old male with no other health issues did well, but would an 80-year-old patient have tolerated the poorly coordinated teamwork without some untoward outcome, such as a stroke? After all our excellent progress in improving process and patient outcomes in the IHI Collaborative, why should we flounder?

(continued on page 94)

Personal Experience with the Use of Checklists in Cardiac Surgery (continued)

Although I have been a pilot since the 1970s, I had never used a simple, aviation-style checklist when taking a patient off bypass support. I decided that night that even though our teams were very experienced in cardiac surgery, I wanted the teams involved in the surgical cases that I would perform to use a simple checklist before we came off bypass.When we separate from bypass, the surgeon, the anesthesiologist, and the technician (perfusionist) operating the bypass equipment each thinks he or she is in charge, but perhaps in reality no one is functionally in charge. If this is the case, is that not a time of high and unacceptable risk for our patients?

The following day I discussed this with several perfusionists who worked for our surgical group. Each seemed somewhat offended that I would suggest we were missing important issues at a critical time in patient care. Then I shared with them the story from the previous day. I insisted that for cases in which I was the responsible surgeon, I wanted to try using a checklist to make certain the most basic physiologic parameters were met before we subjected the patient to the risk of taking over his or her own circulation. In the face of considerable protest by the perfusionists and the refusal of my surgical partners to adopt a similar practice, we embarked upon a three-month trial using a simple checklist as we separated from bypass.

Our team experience over the following three months was humbling. We quietly acknowledged that we were, on occasion, failing to correct simple parameters that might jeopardize our patients. With little subsequent opposition, our perfusionists adopted the routine use of a simple checklist and became the champions of its use, because we saw that this led to improved outcomes and better care. The use of checklists also led to a healthy respect for new learning and better teamwork.

As I now reflect on my surgical career, I feel appalled that I did not adopt the use of checklists in patient care earlier than 1999, for I had learned of the critical importance of checklist use in aviation two decades earlier. Nevertheless, after the successful implementation of the checklist in the operating room, I subsequently used checklists at other phases of patient care, including at routine six-week postoperative follow-up office visits. I realized that even in the outpatient setting, when I was fatigued, distracted, and busy, I missed simple but important issues in patient care. Today I feel checklists may be used with great benefit at all phases of patient care.

With that said, it should also be emphasized that checklists should not be used without knowledge of how the checklist should be written and without some general knowledge of human factors and crew resource management. Checklists are used inappropriately at times, which can add unnecessary complexity and delay and frustrate team function.

Much of what I have learned about safety in the health care setting, I have learned from models in commercial aviation: human factors, crew resource management, threat and error management, risk and safety management, and safety change processes. The utility of checklists is only one example of a simple tool that health care may learn and adapt from aviation.

to comment about facility design considerations during their careers.

Recently, a new endoscopy center opened with the hope that it would provide better quality of care and efficiency. It was obvious to clinicians during the first days while performing endoscopic procedures that the design of the unit was severely flawed from a safety perspective: The physiologic monitors were located behind the physicians and nurses. Therefore, they could not see physiologic data while caring for their patients. In those circumstances, how can the medical staff provide safe procedural care? This is just one example of a situation where, if medical providers were consulted, the safety procedures could have been designed more effectively.

When physicians are asked to participate on facility design teams, it's likely that they will learn considerably more than they will contribute. However, their ideas about design for functional utility and safety will be invaluable for interdisciplinary design teams and will help prevent flaws such as the one identified in the endoscopy center described above, thus identifying changes that are practical and necessary from a medical point of view.

Most of the energy for design efforts will likely come from architects, administrators, and other members of the design teams. However, physicians will increasingly offer to provide their time for safety initiatives and design efforts, as long as they believe that their patients will benefit and that care delivery efficiencies will improve. To receive wholehearted support and commitment from physicians, potential benefit for both patients *and* providers will need to be high, and the physicians must feel respected and welcomed to the design teams. If investments of time to safety and design teams are unlikely to improve the physician's work life, even if some potential for improved safety exists, medical staff cooperation might remain minimal. Similarly, if a considerable time commitment is required for physician members of design teams, then financial or other compensation should be considered in exchange for the time involved.

There are some specific and practical ways to involve physicians in safety design; the suggestions listed below have all been applied in multiple hospitals and health care organizations throughout the United States. These suggestions might seem familiar in other contexts, but the difference here is the focus on safety in design. Physicians in each setting are being asked, "Do you think this idea, or this design process, or this room design, or this system, *promotes patient safety*?"

1. Active involvement in mock-ups: Encourage physicians to participate in the walk-throughs and comment on the viability of various aspects of the design.
2. Active involvement in the matrix process: Physicians should suggest ways of achieving different design attributes and evaluate their priority.
3. Active involvement and approval of every design phase: Physicians should comment on adjacencies, for example, and on room-by-room schematics.
4. Active involvement in all other process recommendations from the National Learning Lab. Encourage physicians to participate in failure mode and effects analysis, equipment planning, and establishing a checklist for future designs.
5. Active involvement in specific design issues. Encourage physicians to participate in determining the location of wiring in surgical suites, or standardizing outlets, bed controls, storage, and lighting in patient rooms.

6. Active involvement in site visits: Make sure physicians are part of the groups visiting other sites to see how others do it, and get their input on what they see.
7. Formal medical staff structure: Work with the executive committee of the medical staff, keeping them informed and encouraging them to advocate for safety to the rest of the medical staff.
8. Medical directors: Ensure that they are informed advocates to the medical staff also.
9. Physician groups: Attend business meetings of physician groups, particularly where strong relationships with these groups exist, keeping them informed and working through them to their constituents.
10. Board of directors: Physicians are usually members of boards; make sure that communication is clear and constant with all board members, so that they also support the safety design focus.
11. Steering committees: When an organization has formed a steering committee through which ideas flow for safety design projects, make sure that physicians have a voice on the committee.
12. Informal communication: Make a point of keeping up good communication channels between safety design advocates and medical staff, always being open to conversations, ideas, and input from physicians in more informal settings outside structured committees.

Physicians, like most others, dislike being told what to do. In organizational settings where effective leadership is modeled, being told what to do rarely occurs. Rather, an environment of respectful listening, shared learning, and leading by questions is often found. Increased likelihood for collaboration around safety culture and facility design will flourish where mutual respect and trust are evident each day. Contributions by team members should be shared, appreciated, respected, and acknowledged. Enthusiasm grows in such environments. Taking responsibility for one's relationships with others on safety and design teams is necessary for success. As Peter Drucker advises, "Listen first, speak last."[29]

Leadership, Trust, and Values

Health care today is interesting, challenging, and exciting. The era of blind trust in care providers has ended, and has been replaced by transparency in performance and outcomes. The focus on safety will become visible to all constituents. Pay for providers may slowly become based on some measures of performance, if financial incentives prove effective stimulus for quality and safety.[30] The changes and challenges in health care over the past several decades have been complex and nonlinear, and the sheer complexity may seem to keep people on the edge of chaos, but right there is where the best creativity may reside.

Leadership
Effective leadership is key to providing large-scale improvement in safety culture, yet the requirements for new leadership are radically different from our traditional health care leadership models. The chief role of leadership may be to mobilize our collective capacities to challenge difficult circumstances. An excellent example of this can be found in the "harmonization" of safety practices in 2006 by the National Quality Forum–sponsored, interorganizational sharing and learning between The Joint Commission, the CMS, the IHI, the Leapfrog Group, and AHRQ.[31] This "harmonization," or standardization, of safety practices should simplify standards for hospital safety committees and CEOs, as well as for certifying, purchasing, and quality organizations.

As change occurs, emotional tensions rise. As emotional tension intensifies, leadership becomes more important. Leadership is required for those problems without easy solutions and that require new information and learning. Leaders must foster daily opportunities for new individual and collective learning and model the learning they expect of others.

To be most effective, learning must occur in the context of daily organizational operations. New knowledge must be shared throughout organizations, and leaders must help remove obstacles to the sharing of new knowledge. New learning must be recognized, appreciated, and rewarded. Modeling and mentoring by leaders at all levels of our organizations should be expected and valued.

Part of leadership is accountability, or being responsible, and physician accountability in endorsing and supporting what evidence-based medicine deems best care is extremely important. Although some might not consider themselves leaders, they are, in fact, considered leaders by junior colleagues, ancillary staff, and patients. While speaking at the University of Miami on the subject of "Perspectives on Patient Safety and Quality Lessons from IHI's 100,000 Lives Campaign," Don Berwick, M.D., president and CEO of IHI, acknowledged three factors that are usually involved when safety initiatives are a success: standardization, the presence of a "clinical champion" for the initiative, and accountability.[32] Remembering the importance of accountability and demonstrating responsible behavior are essential.

One current example of poor physician accountability seen in many hospitals is the inadequate compliance with hand washing by physicians between patient visits. Although hand washing is important for decreasing health care–associated infections, not all physicians are consistently "on board" with this practice.

In his book *Leading in a Culture of Change,* Michael Fullan stresses that producing sustainable performance requires leadership at all levels of our organizations. Developing such pervasive leadership talent may occur after mastering five core competencies: moral purpose, understanding the change process, building relationships, knowledge building, and coherence making as a "remarkable convergence" of competencies for leaders in complex times.[33] Julianne Morath, a nationally recognized leader in patient safety, recipient of the John M. Eisenberg Patient Safety Award, and chief operating officer of the Minneapolis Children's Hospital and Clinics, has said:

> What we do is orient the whole organization and its operations around the platform of patient safety. That is job number one for our leaders. From that, everything else flows. . . . Patient safety must be hardwired into expectations of all our job descriptions, in our incentives, in our credentialing, our continuing education, our orientation.[31(p. 230)]

Trust

A discussion of leadership would be incomplete without mention of the importance of trust. Leaders must continually model trust and foster environments of trust both within and outside their organizations. Unfortunately, efforts in attempting to build trust often produce the opposite effect by pointing out how little trust actually exists in organizations. Trust is earned only over time; no shortcuts exist. Trust results from saying what we do and doing what we say continually over a long time. The evolution of a trusting organizational environment provides the foundation for the mutual sharing of information and knowledge that is critical for sustained success. Trust within and across hospital design and other teams is critically important.

The research of Daniel Kim on efficiency and effectiveness in automobile manufacturing can have an interesting application to health care safety design. When studying auto design teams that worked on the development of different automotive systems, Kim learned that quick fixes for one team often created new problems for other teams, which eventually led to feelings of antagonism and distrust and resulted in considerable design rework in the end. Thus, although quick fixes may have simply solved one team's challenge, the results were often counterproductive for the organization. Particularly harmful was the erosion of trust between teams.[34] Had more time been devoted initially to collaboration and developing trust across teams, gains in efficiency, shared learning, and production output might have occurred. This is likely as true in health care environments as it is in the automobile industry.

Values

Health care leaders must also develop, share, and live their values. Every phase of organizational function needs to be developed around values. Leaders must learn how to discuss their values, embrace them, and have the courage to hire and fire within the organization based on shared values. How common it is to see or hear of organizations that espouse but do not live their values. When people fail to live by their values, then integrity, trust, and learning are eroded and organizational success and sustainability flounder. The science of health care safety is young, and "the road to hospital patient safety is long and complicated."[10(p.2864)] Leaders in health care facility design and innovators of safety initiatives may be wise to heed Schein's advice that "in the end, cultural understanding and cultural learning starts with self insight."[27(p.418)]

Summary

The concept of physician involvement in hospitals designed for safety is exciting and novel. Interdisciplinary team approaches for design have strong external validity and are encouraged by similar models of interdisciplinary design in other industries. Hopefully there will soon be preliminary data that will link safety outcomes with the structure and process of new hospitals designed for safety.

New learning about safety culture by health care professions cannot be forced; it must be nurtured. Physicians are critical components in moving ahead with safety culture and designs for safety, for they work at the "sharp end" of care delivery. Their input, creative thinking, and innovations as health care leaders are imperative. Without such participation the movement toward safety initiatives and a culture of safety will fail.

The road to health care safety is long and the challenges multiple and complex. Some progress has occurred in the six years since the IOM report on errors in health care, although many believe that the progress made has been modest at best. The era of blind trust of medical providers has ended. A new era of transparency has arrived in which the structures, processes, outcomes of care, and focus on safety by providers and institutions will be visible to all constituents. With this new era will come continual change, great challenges for innovation, and wonderful opportunities to learn together.

Physicians have moved slowly and cautiously to join the safety movement. Explanations for the slow transition to safety culture are believable and should be respected. Acknowledging the magnitude of problems in patient safety has been difficult for many physicians, and truly internalizing such acknowledgment, once made, has been challenging. Lack of consistent nomenclature about error and the lack of data about positive outcomes from recommended safety fixes has slowed adaptation of safety culture. Diversity in beliefs and values around the importance of safety initiatives has slowed adaptation and added complexity. Failure of many recommended changes in health care models over the previous decade, such as horizontal and vertical integration of care, and consolidation of business management models, have made physicians reluctant to endorse new recommendations, as has the perpetual concern and potential threat of medical malpractice litigation.

Physicians currently face numerous challenges. Although most providers feel gratitude for the opportunity to serve mankind, many are stressed, chronically fatigued, harbor little resilience, and have minimal reserve for listening to patients. Many have reached their limits of "running faster" and "doing more." Yet providers are continually being asked to provide more care for patients with fewer and fewer resources of time, personnel, and money. Many physicians are angry. In such environments, one finds degradation in effective communications, teamwork, and safety, as well as the isolation of practitioners, and disharmony among medical staff and between physicians and hospital administrations. These and other factors in the current health care environment are counterproductive to promoting safety.

There is a dramatic need for new, strong, effective leadership by health care professionals during these times of transition to a culture of safety. New leadership will need training in educational skills largely unknown to our predecessors, such as teamwork, improving communications, knowledge about human factors, risk and safety management systems, and threat and error management. All physicians will need some exposure and training in these new concepts. Leadership must foster organizations in which new learning occurs in the context of daily operation and is respected and shared throughout the organization. Also, leadership must model values of learning and trust, provide mentorship for leaders at all levels of the organizational structure, and stress the importance of accountability.

Courage, strength, and determination are needed to foster true commitment to the culture of safety. Progress must also be made in other areas of health care besides safety that contribute to the ongoing fragmentation and demise of the health care system. Progress in improving safety culture will remain meager if solutions in corruption, better balancing of funding priorities, legislative support, fair reimbursement for injury, and other major issues are not successfully engaged.

A healing and caring culture of safety *can* exist in health care. And physicians *will* be part of this new safety culture because, despite obstacles and difficulties, physicians in the end want not only more efficient care, but also what is best for their patients and their families. Safer care is better, more efficient care.

References

1. Piergeorge A.R., Cesarona F.L., Casanova D.M.: Designing the critical care unit: A multidisciplinary approach. *Crit Care Med* 11(7):541–545, 1983.

2. Swaim T.: Staff involvement in critical care unit construction. *Crit Care Nurs Q* 14(1):63–70, 1991.

3. Guidelines for Intensive Care Unit Design. Guidelines/Practice Parameters Committee of the American College of Critical Care Medicine, Society of Critical Care Medicine. *Crit Care Med* 23(3):582–588, 1995.

4. Marshall M. Jr.: The physician's role in health facility planning. *Pa Med* 70(6):81–82, 1967.

5. Reiling J.G., et al.: Enhancing the traditional hospital design process: A focus on patient safety. *Jt Comm J Qual Saf* 30(3):115–124, 2004.

6. Marck P.B., et al.: Building safer systems by ecological design: using restoration science to develop a medication safety intervention. *Qual Saf Health Care* 15(2):92–97, 2006.

7. Dickerman K.N., Nevo I., Barach P.: Incorporating patient-safe design into the guidelines. *Journal of the American Institute of Architecture* Oct. 19, 2005.

8. Rashid M.: A decade of adult intensive care unit design: A study of the physical design features of the best-practice examples. *Crit Care Nurs Q* 29(4):282–311, 2006.

9. Institute of Medicine: *Crossing the Quality Chasm: A New Health System for the 21st Century* Washington, DC: National Academy Press, 2001.

10. Longo D.R., et al.: The long road to patient safety. *JAMA* 294(22):2858–2865, 2005.

11. Wachter R.M., Shojania K.G.: *Internal Bleeding: The Truth Behind America's Terrifying Epidemic of Medical Mistakes,* 2nd ed. New York: Rugged Land, LLC, 2004.

12. *Adverse Health Events in Minnesota—Third Annual Report.* St. Paul, Minnesota Department of Health, 2007.

13. Schein E.H.: *Career Anchors: Self Assessment,* 3rd ed. San Francisco: Pfeiffer, 2006.

14. Senge P.S., et al.: *Presence: Human Purpose and the Field of the Future,* Cambridge, MA: The Society for Organizational Learning, Inc., 2004,.

15. Personal communication between the author and Edmund J. Makoski, M.D., Atlanta, Feb. 2006.

16. Rosenthal M.M., Sutcliffe K.M. (eds): *Medical Error—What Do We Know? What Do We Do?* San Francisco: Jossey-Bass, 2002, p. 325.

17. Blendon R.J., et al.: Views of practicing physicians and the public on medical errors. *N Eng J Med* 347(24):1933–1940, 2002.

18. Winters B.D., Pham J., Pronovost P.J.: Rapid response teams—Walk, don't run. *JAMA* 296(13):1645–1647, 2006.

19. Pronovost P.J., Miller M.R., Wachter R.M.: Tracking progress in patient safety. *JAMA* 296(6):696–699, 2006.

20. Fonarow G.C., et al.: Association between performance measures and clinical outcomes for patients hospitalized with heart failure. *JAMA* 297(1):61–70, 2007.

21. Agency for Healthcare Research and Quality: *Hospital Survey on Patient Safety Culture Database.* http://www.ahrq.gov/qual/hospculture/ (accessed Mar. 14, 2007).

22. Lindenauer P.K., et al.: Public reporting and pay for performance in hospital quality improvement. *N Eng J Med* 356(5):515–517, 2007.

23. Sandy L.G.: Homeostasis without reserve—The risk of health system collapse. *N Eng J Med* 347(24):1971–1975, 2002.

24. Cameron K.S., Quinn R.E.: *Diagnosing and Changing Organizational Culture: Based on the Competing Values Framework,* rev. ed. San Francisco: Jossey-Bass, 2006.

25. Personal communication between the author and Bruce G. Tesmer and Robert L. Helmreich, Austin, TX, Jan. 2006.

26. Herzlinger R.E.: Why innovation in health care is so hard. *Har Bus Rev* 84(5):58–66, 2006.

27. Schein E.H.: *Organizational Culture and Leadership,* 3rd ed. San Francisco: Jossey-Bass, 2004.

28. Turner K.: *Integrated Risk and Safety Management.* Sydney, Australia: The Aerosafe Group, 2006.

29. Drucker P.F.: What executives should remember. *Har Bus Rev* 84(2):144–153, 166, 2006.

30. Epstein A.M.: Pay for performance at the tipping point. *N Eng J Med* 356(5):515–517, 2007.

31. Denham C.R.: From harmony to healing: Join the quality choir. *Journal of Patient Safety* 2:225–232, Dec. 2006.

32. Personal communication between John Reiling and Donald Berwick, M.D., Miami, Oct. 18, 2006.

33. Fullan M.: *Leading in a Culture of Change.* San Francisco: Jossey-Bass, 2001.

34. Roth G.: *Car Launch: The Human Side of Managing Change.* New York: Oxford University Press, 1999.

Chapter 8

Putting It All Together: A Case Study of One Organization's Use of the National Learning Lab Recommendations

"People of good intention, skilled and experienced, may nonetheless be forced to commit errors by the way in which the design of their environment calls forth their behavior." (Neville Moray, "Error Reduction as a Systems Problem," in *Human Error in Medicine*, ed. Marilyn Sue Bogner. Hillsdale, NJ: Lawrence Erlbaum Associates, 1994, pp. 67–91.)

After the National Learning Lab developed its recommendations for safety in design, the first hospital to implement these recommendations in designing a new facility was St. Joseph's Hospital in West Bend, Wisconsin. This chapter describes how the St. Joseph's design team implemented the design concepts. The description is not meant to provide a blueprint; rather, it provides an example of how to practically apply the National Learning Lab recommendations.

The single-patient rooms at St. Joseph's evolved over months of design. The design process involved employees, physicians, board members, administration, National Learning Lab participants, expert consultants, other health systems, health care writers, and design teams. More than 27 different designs or refinements were made on the room. Failure mode and effects analysis (FMEA), patient focus groups, mock-ups with employee evaluation, and checklist safety design principles (latent conditions and active failures) helped St. Joseph's create the safest rooms they could envision.

This style is not the only way a patient room can be designed for safety; there are multiple ways to do this. However, the design exhibits efficient, thoughtful features that meet National Learning Lab expectations. Patient rooms such as those in use at St. Joseph's illustrate how process recommendations were helpful in focusing on safety in design. Front-line employees were active in the design, and their feedback was heard. In addition, safety culture was affected by the process of focusing on safety in design of the patient rooms because of the extensive involvement of employees, physicians, and the community.

Single-Patient Room

The floor plan shown in Figure 8-1 on page 102 illustrates how a series of standardized single-patient rooms are laid out on both sides of a hallway in St. Joseph's Hospital. They may be the first truly standardized patient rooms in any hospital in the United States.

Figure 8-2, page 103, which shows the interior of a single-patient room, is an example of how many of the latent conditions and active failures recommendations in the design for safety were met and combined into an attractive and efficient single-patient room.

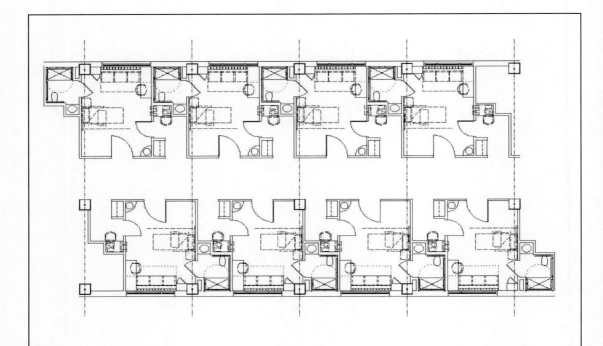

Figure 8-1. Floor Plan of Standardized Patient Rooms, St. Joseph's Hospital, West Bend, Wisconsin.

Source: St. Joseph's Hospital, West Bend, WI. Used with permission.

The "bird's eye view" perspective in Figure 8-2 allows various features of the room to be seen in relation to each other. Notice the two entrances to the room, one from the hallway (along the lower edge of the picture), and one from the alcove on the right. In the alcove, which is also entered from the hallway, a desk, a computer, and a chair are available for staff use. The alcove also contains a standardized storage area so that staff can find everything they need to care for the patient adjacent to the patient room. The family area is in the right corner of the room, by the window, and includes a couch/pullout bed, a chair, a desk with Internet connection, and natural lighting. The treatment area of the room is on the left side of the bed, with room around the bed for patient care. It is intentional that the patient is on the caregiver's right as that person enters the room from either door, so that care can be provided more efficiently. Note that the bathroom is at the head of the patient's bed, allowing the patient to get to and from the bathroom without impediments, holding onto a rail if necessary. At the head of the bed is a standardized headwall with connections for various gases such as oxygen; on the wall to the left of the bed is a pull-down table the caregiver can use. Although it is not shown in the illustration, there is also a "COW" (computer on wheels) in each room. In the lower right-hand corner of the room (not visible in the illustration), between the two doorways and easily visible to the patient, is a sink, an ever-present and convenient reminder to staff and visitors to wash their hands.

Figure 8-2. Single-Patient Room, St. Joseph's Hospital, West Bend, Wisconsin.

Source: St. Joseph's Hospital, West Bend, WI. Used with permission.

Latent Conditions and Active Failures

Many of the design features that focused on latent conditions and active failures were incorporated at St. Joseph's. The patient room was selected as a good example of how the design plan for the hospital came together in one location. To show how the room design was reached, each of the applicable latent conditions and active failures will be discussed, to explain how they relate to the plan for a single-patient room.

Latent Conditions

The design team determined which structural system to use and reviewed the benefits of steel versus concrete. Concrete minimizes vibration noise but is less scalable, adaptable, and flexible than steel. A higher-strength steel can meet these three criteria, but it can possibly interfere with wireless technologies and thereby hinder staff's ability to provide immediate information close to the patient. Steel is

---

The Move Toward Single-Patient Rooms

The 2006 edition of the *Guidelines for Design and Construction of Health Care Facilities,* by the Facilities Guidelines Institute and published by the American Institute of Architects, states that single-patient rooms in medical/surgical units and postpartum units should become standard in all newly constructed hospitals.

Numerous studies have shown that single-patient rooms can reduce medical errors; lower potential for disease transmission, including infections; reduce privacy violations; prevent patient falls; and reduce risk for patients.[1]

According to a report in the *Wall Street Journal*, private rooms can also reduce a hospital's operating costs. Although private rooms can initially cost more to build, their savings in long-term operational costs can offset the initial investment. Patients tend to recover faster in private rooms, they are less susceptible to disease transmission, and they are more likely to receive the correct medication because potential confusion with a roommate is eliminated. Patients also don't have to contend with disturbances from care providers attending to a roommate or visits from a roommate's family.[2]

Bronson Methodist Hospital in Kalamazoo, Michigan, saw a 45% decline in infection rates in its new hospital, which has private rooms, compared with its older facility, which had semiprivate rooms. The private rooms in Bronson's new facility cost more to build, but their savings in operational costs from the reduced infection rates offset the original capital.[2]

References
1. American Institute of Architects: *Private Rooms Are New Standard in* Updated Guidelines for Design and Construction of Health Care Facilities. Jul. 19, 2006.
   http://www.aia.org/print_template.cfm?pagename=release_071906_healthcare (accessed May 30, 2007).
2. Landro L.: New standards for hospitals call for patients to get private rooms. *Wall Street Journal* p. A1, Mar. 22, 2006.

---

also less expensive than cement. Therefore, St. Joseph's decided to use a higher-strength steel than is typically used in hospitals and, in addition, designed cement pods between floors to reduce vibration. This solution assured the technology experts that the wireless concerns could be fully resolved.

The design team determined that ceiling heights would be 9 to 10 feet high, thereby allowing the scalability and adaptability criteria to be met. Higher ceiling heights allow future new technologies or upgrades in current technologies to be accessible. For example, it will be possible in future patient rooms to have tracks for radiology equipment so that services can be brought to the patient rather than taking the patient to radiology, thus eliminating transfers and their hand offs. The design team used the matrix exercise (*see* pages 35–37 in Chapter 4) to make decisions having an impact on patient safety by meeting latent conditions or active failures changes.

Noise reduction

A standardized patient room has material effects on noise. The bed is in the same location in each room. In the traditional patient room style, called "back-to-back," patient beds are on the same wall. Back-to-back plans create significant transfer noise between rooms. In addition, many of these rooms use the same oxygen, nitrogen, and suction sources, which intensify the transfer noise and vibration. This does not occur in a standardized room. Also, the walls between rooms are separated and insulated with an airspace that minimizes transfer noise. The steel structure was designed specifically to allow for standardization. In addition, vibration noise between floors and within floors is minimized through design. The mechanical, electrical, and plumbing systems were designed to use the best materials for minimizing noise. Mechanical air-handling systems also were designed to reduce noise.

The flooring in the patient rooms is made of rubber. Although carpet is quieter than rubber and it was mocked up and tested, the design team did not select carpet as the flooring material because spills and mishaps on carpet need to be cleaned up immediately. Carpet spills also necessitate the use of carpet cleaner, which could take time to get and also could be embarrassing for patients. However, for the alcoves and hallways the design team chose carpet with a low nap specifically for use in hospitals.

The team also selected special ceiling tiles that absorb noise better than regular ceiling tiles. Triple-glazed windows were installed to minimize outside noises. No overhead paging system is used—with one exception, for an emergency fire alarm—and nurse call systems use vibrating features. As specific equipment and technologies were needed, one important criterion the design team used was to ask the manufacturers of the specific piece of equipment or technology how they reduced noise in their products.

Scalability, adaptability, flexibility
All rooms have higher than normal ceilings to allow future changes to be incorporated more easily. Space around the bed is sized so that in the future, procedures such as colonoscopies can be performed in the room. The standardized rooms on the third floor of St. Joseph's could be duplicated on a fourth floor, and infrastructure and elevators have been sized to add this floor.

Visibility of patients to staff
In each patient room, the alcove door has a window with a blind so that nurses working in the alcove can see the patient. The nurse can also check on the patient in the evening without opening the door and waking the patient. The caregiver can complete services to a patient one at a time, with visual control, before providing services to another patient. Each room is wired for cameras to allow observation. All materials, such as medication, linens, IV poles, and a rough-in for ice makers, are delivered to the room to allow nurses to spend more time with the patient. The patient's chart will initially be in the room but will be replaced with electronic medical records (EMRs). A work space allows nurses and other caregivers to spend more time with the patient.

Visibility also means lighting to see the patient. Natural light is maximized by large windows in every patient room. Light sources after hours are as close to natural light as can be achieved cost-effectively. Sixteen lights are located in every room, including the bathroom and alcoves. Canned lights are located over the patient to allow for assessment. Bathroom lights turn on by motion sensors, allowing caregivers to stay focused on helping patients instead of reaching for a light switch.

Patients involved with their care
Each patient room is designed with a treatment section near the door and a family section near the window. A couch folds out into a bed; a desk with Internet connection encourages family members or friends to stay with the patient. This will help patients to be more active with care and therefore better able to protect themselves from errors. A portable computer on a cart will be located in each room so patients can have appropriate access to their charts (the Medication Activity Report, for example), as the charts become automated.

Standardization
The patient rooms in St. Joseph's may be the first patient rooms in the country to be truly standardized. The headwalls and material drawers are standardized throughout the facility. The EMR, bar coding, computerized prescriber order entry (CPOE), and other technologies will be standardized eventually, assisting in the development of standardized protocols and order sets. The facility materials distribution and routine nurse functions can also be standardized to match the facility. Mechanical, electrical, and plumbing systems are standardized so repairs and maintenance can be accurate, simplified, and cost-effective.

One of the hospital's goals is to fully standardize equipment to provide the highest level of safety. The complexity and variety in equipment vendors and models is immense, and such complexity creates more errors. This lack of equipment standardization was repeatedly identified as a failure during one of the design team's design FMEA (dFMEA) exercises (*see* pages 38–44 in Chapter 4 for more information on dFMEA). As a result, St. Joseph's is moving toward equipment standardization. For example, a vendor for a specific product monitor is determined; then, as products are replaced or upgraded, they are replaced with the standardized choice.

Automation where possible
Automatic medical records, bar coding, CPOE, pneumatic tubes, two computers in every room (one in the alcove and one on a cart in the room), a sophisticated nurse call system, new patient beds, and patient lifts for every room are examples of automation. These applications will allow caregivers to provide care more efficiently and rely less on short-term memory.

Many design features and technology applications have affected multiple latent conditions. This was one of the important criteria used during the matrix exercise (*see* pages 35–37 in Chapter 4 for more information) to determine which design features to include. Technology applications were deemed to be a critical part of allowing St. Joseph's to design for safety.

Minimizing fatigue
Using carpet and rubber flooring, placing a chair in patient room alcoves, having single-patient rooms, keeping all materials in patient room alcoves so nurses take fewer steps while caring for patients, relying less on short-term memory, having less noise, incorporating natural light into patient rooms, and using strong lighting sources can help organizations lower fatigue among staff.

Immediate accessibility of information, close to the point of service
EMRs are a useful way of making information accessible quickly at the point of service. Allowing fam-

ily members to stay with patients will also help, as will keeping the paper chart in the alcove until the EMR is implemented.

Minimizing patient transfers/hand offs

Private single rooms with space around the beds will allow as many procedures to be performed in the room as possible, such as obstetrics and Labor Delivery Recovery Postpartum rooms where the mother delivers a baby and the baby can stay with the mother in the same room for the entire stay. EMRs are another important tool in minimizing data hand offs as staff changes or patients are moved. Bar coding helps with continually identifying the patient.

Active Failures

Although nine active failures were identified during the National Learning Lab, only eight are relevant to the design of a patient room and will be discussed below.

Operative/postoperative complications/infections

Features to minimize infection include the following:

- Private rooms
- A sink in the main room that staff must pass before going into either door
- No blinds on windows
- HEPA filters
- Ultraviolet lights in all patient areas
- Airflow systems in which clean air passes the patient and is recycled and filtered
- A fan for windows to minimize condensation

Stainless-steel grates that require cleaning have been upgraded to help minimize infections. However, the most important design element is the location of the sink, as lack of hand washing is the leading cause of hospital-acquired infections.

Inpatient suicides

Data from The Joint Commission indicate that out of the approximately 1,500 to 1,800 suicides that occur in hospitals, approximately 50% occur on medical/surgical units. The two most common methods are jumping and hanging. Suicidal patients have access to many things to use during a suicide attempt while in a medical/surgical room, such as bathroom curtain rods, showerheads, television brackets, or lights.

As a result, St. Joseph's decided to use breakaway shower curtain rods and minimize other hanging risks by choosing lights and brackets that met the design of the room but would be less likely to be used for a suicide attempt. To minimize jumping from a window, windows are no longer able to be opened and are triple-paned, making them more difficult to break through. If a patient is identified as being at risk for suicide, the patient is transferred to the mental health unit, while at the same time increased visibility in all patient rooms helps staff keep a closer watch, helping to minimize the risk of suicides.

Incorrect tube—incorrect connector—incorrect hole placement events/oxygen cylinder hazards

All connectors are color coded and are a different size for each different gas. Storage and identification of portable gases also use this approach. In addition, all gases are in standardized locations to minimize the risk of a gas-connecting error.

Medication error–related events/transfusion-related events

Bar coding, unit doses at the point of service, EMR, and CPOE are critical elements for reducing medication errors. Private rooms with alcoves that include medical records allow nurses to concentrate on one patient and document efforts on the same patient before moving to the next patient.

Deaths of patients in restraints/patient falls

Like most hospitals, St. Joseph's has minimized the use of restraints. The new beds for the hospital have eliminated many of the risks of restraint-related deaths. However, a decreased use of restraints has led to an increased risk of falls. Using beds that drop down to 16 inches above the floor and placing the bathroom at the head of the bed, with railings to the stool and shower, are design elements that can reduce falls. Most patients fall at night or while walking with a nurse or other caregiver. Other features designed to minimize falls include an automated light in the bathroom, windows in patient doors and wiring for cameras to increase staff's visibility of the patient, and allowing family members to stay in the patient's room.

Chapter 9
Implementing Safe by Design: Overcoming Resistance and Achieving Success

"Hospitals pose many challenges to those undertaking reform of health care systems. They are quite literally, immovable structures whose design. . . .reflects the practice of health care and the patient populations of a bygone era." (Martin McKee and Judith Healy, "The Role of the Hospital in a Changing Environment," *Bulletin of the World Health Organization* 78(6), 2000, p. 803.)

Practically speaking, what does it take to reach the goal of designing a hospital with its equipment and technology which is focused on patient safety? The first part of this chapter answers this question and identifies three necessary components for success: leadership, a common belief, and an understanding of the National Learning Lab's recommendations and what various stakeholders can contribute to the recommendations. The second part of the chapter identifies why change is difficult and how resistance can be a barrier to effective design.

Many stakeholders are involved in the creation of a new or remodeled hospital. The stakeholders include the owner's representative (an external consultant experienced in building projects who represents the hospital as it interfaces with the external design team), general contractors, architects, mechanical/electrical/plumbing architects, equipment planners, vendors, specialty consultants (such as a dietary consultant), the board of directors, the president/CEO, management staff, volunteers, medical staff, patients and families, and the community. Each of these stakeholders approaches the facility development process with a different set of expectations, although many overlap. Historically, however, these stakeholders have never approached a facility development process while using patient safety as their driving principle. It is not an easy task to begin the process of change within a hospital. As McKee and Healy state: "Hospitals pose many challenges to those undertaking reform of health care systems. They are quite literally, immovable structures whose design was set in concrete, usually many years previously. Their configuration often reflects the practice of health care and the patient populations of a bygone era."[1(p.803)]

Requirements for Effective Design

Any attempt to gain the support of all the stakeholders involved in facility development to reach consensus on safety in design demands good leadership, the sharing of a common belief system, a clear understanding of the National Learning Lab recommendations, and the realization that each stakeholder can indeed contribute to this design.

Leadership
The ability to design by safety and to enhance a safety culture demands strong leadership from management, the board, physicians, and design teams. The hospital CEO's understanding and commitment to the goal of designing a safe hospital and enhancing a safety culture is essential. The CEO sets the culture for the organization and influences the board, the medical staff, and the design team.

Physicians also must show leadership. Brent T. James, M.D., vice president of Research and executive director, Intermountain Healthcare, for Healthcare Delivery Research, Salt Lake City, has a theory he describes as "the square root of **n**." He believes that to enhance safety culture and develop safe practices and policies, the number of physician leaders committed to change needs to be the square root of the number of active medical staff. Ongoing strategies employed by medical staff committed to change include continuing to identify physician leaders, involving them in continuing education on patient-safe design, involving them early in the design process, and providing economic and efficiency incentives to be active in safety and quality initiatives.[2] (*See* Chapter 7 for more on the role of the medical staff.)

Leadership from the design team, particularly architects, is also a critical element for a successful safe-by-design process. Other important team members include mechanical/electrical/plumbing architects and the principal designers. The owner's representative, equipment planners, specialty consultants, equipment and technology vendors, and general contractors can all influence the success of safety by design. Architects particularly influence employees and physicians, as employees and physicians "buy into" safety design principles and suggest ways to apply them. (*See* Chapter 6 for more on the role of architects in safe by design.)

Leadership is also required from the rest of the design team, which includes point-of-care staff and management working with architects to design spaces. As discussed in Chapter 2, astronauts will not let architects and engineers design their spaces without input from the astronauts themselves. It is critical to the success of the space mission that the design reflects their requirements. Hospital design teams must have the same attitude. Hospital architects do not work everyday in the spaces they design. The human factors, latent conditions, and active failures found in hospital settings are understood and felt by the staff. To create a hospital designed and focused on safety demands input from everyone on the design teams.

Common Belief

Common belief is emotional and data driven. In health care, stakeholders need to know and feel the effects that the harm caused by medical error can have on patients, families, and staff. Chapter 3 discusses strategies to develop common belief among staff and physicians. However, common belief is more difficult to achieve for board members, the design team, patients and their families, and the community. Many in these groups believe that hospitals should be, and therefore are, inherently safe. In addition, many architects believe that they have always designed "safe" hospitals. On the other hand, for some board members who have been involved with the hospital for years, safety had not ever been identified as a serious issue. As a result, a commonly held position is "errors do not happen here"—that is, in one's own institution—or if they did, they could not be fixed simply by changing facility design.

However, some of these stakeholders have been personally affected by preventable adverse events; others have become aware of them through their place of work or through family or friends. Encouraging such stories to surface, along with stories from other hospitals, helps raise awareness of the importance of safe design. This, coupled with the data from numerous studies, is an important part of the education process that must occur to ensure that a common belief around safe design is developed.

Patients, their families, and the community are especially complicated stakeholder groups to bring together with a shared belief. One reason is that the strategy of advertising or holding public forums to discuss the level of harm happening in hospitals, and how that is partly a result of latent conditions and active failures, is risky. The hospital could alienate its ultimate customers, who might decide it would be risky for them to go to that particular hospital if so much harm occurs there. Most people think hospitals are inherently safe because competent, caring nurses, physicians, and other caregivers practice in them. Patients and their families might question their confidence in the caregivers or lose trust in the care provided. One way to address this issue is to organize focus groups to educate people about the National Learning Lab recommendations. If mock-ups are available, the focus groups can be asked to evaluate them. The hospital's advertising could stress that the enhancements in its facilities will improve quality and safety, possibly positioning the hospital as a leading-edge care provider. Acknowledging the issue of safety while simultaneously describing solutions to safety-related issues is another recognized approach. It is also important to note that society is becoming more educated on preventable adverse events in hospitals.

Understanding National Learning Lab Recommendations and Realizing Stakeholders' Contributions

Understanding the significance of latent conditions and active failures and how they affect safe design demands an understanding of human error and the causes of cognitive failure (*see* Chapter 1). Education, discussions, and debates are critical. It is important to encourage stakeholders to review the research on harm, and then, if possible, see the actual effects of that harm. Following the process design recommendations from the National Learning Lab is useful to gaining an understanding of latent conditions and active failures. Understanding the recommendations will deepen as the design process unfolds, through interaction with processes such as matrix development, failure mode and effects analysis (FMEA), and mock-ups.

Each stakeholder can contribute to safe design. Truly, safety is in everybody's hands. All stakeholders, whether they are board members, nurses, physicians, or architects, could initially minimize the impact they think they can have. But as the design process unfolds, the stakeholders' level of commitment, insight, and creativity will increase to meet the National Learning Lab requirements. Although everyone brings different expertise to the table, all expertise is needed.

Barriers to Effective Design

Barriers to effective design can include fear of capital overruns as a result of safety design features or not having enough capital for technology, equipment, and facility features; concerns about the business case for safety; concerns about whether the safety design will have the desired effect; the money market/hospital culture; differences in common belief; the medical model of individual perfection, as opposed to the concept of a just culture; the lack of robust evidence-based practices such as standardized order sets; apprehension about the amount of change required; lack of awareness of the great opportunity that lies ahead; and finally, concerns about leadership.

Barriers such as a common belief and a just culture have been explored previously in Chapter 3, which discusses the need for strong leadership, as well as apprehension about change and lack of awareness of future possibilities. The money market/hospital culture and evidence-based practices such as standardized order sets are discussed below. (Chapter 10 will discuss the business case for patient safety and management of capital for safety features, including technology and equipment.)

Most health care administrators focus on money and market. Without market share, competitive positions may be eroded, leading to less volume, which leads to an eroding financial condition. Strong or adequate financial results are essential to the survival of any hospital—no margin, no mission. Boards of directors are also generally focused on this issue. Financial results and market share are key components of most health care management incentive packages. To introduce safety as a major focus for the organization causes a significant shift in organizational focus. Balanced scorecards, changes in incentive programs, board meeting changes, executive team discussions focused on safety, and executive walk-arounds are all ways to integrate safety into the money market/hospital culture.

But changing the money market/culture barrier does not always address the concern, Will it work? Time and patience are required. To their knowledge, St. Joseph's Hospital was the first hospital in the country to focus on safety in design, and it didn't officially open until August 2005. Other health care organizations are following suit. But even if it is possible to show many safety improvements, we will never know completely if the improvements are a direct result of safety in design or if other factors are involved. However, it simply makes practical sense to have safety in design in health care, if the business case requirements are met.

A hospital's medical staff will likely have many concerns in addition to the question of whether safe design works. Lack of a common belief and a just culture is a barrier to physician engagement in a design process focused on safety. A related issue for physicians is standardization due to evidence-based medicine, which conflicts with the traditional autonomy and independence of physicians. Individual physicians are responsible for clinical decisions and the quality of those decisions. Clinical quality for many physicians means making perfect decisions. Recognizing what effect systems and facilities can have on quality and safety is difficult for many physicians to internalize. It is this individualistic training and behavior that keeps them from accepting the opportunity to enhance safety through design and see the need for standardization.

Another concern of the medical staff is the financial impact of safety by design. The financial system provides incentives to physicians to perform procedures one-on-one with patients, rather than encouraging goals such as team behavior and the creation of processes that reduce procedures. Safety by design can have a positive impact on efficiency; however, this can influence physician buy-in.

Many hospitals never undertake planning for a completely new facility, even when remodeling has occurred multiple times. If the hospital has existed on its site for many years, the staff is often quite stable, with many employees having worked there a long time. A stable staff leads to stable processes. The recognition of the patient safety issue, the opportunity to affect safety through design, and learning to design around safety, including its technology and equipment changes, create immense change. Managing the change and overcoming the change barrier will be two of the most challenging issues for management. Besides coping with the changes they are personally going through, management must also support the changes being experienced by all employees and physicians in the organization.

The platform for change is there. Every process that every employee uses will change as a hospital relocates or remodels and as people cope with new spaces, new technology, and new equipment. The realization that safety is a major concern is another critical change platform. Although that platform for change exists, actually making the changes is difficult. The work load of designing a new facility focused on safety, while at the same time providing care to patients, can sometimes seem overwhelming. Staff can be encouraged to focus on current operations while accepting the impending changes, even when this may require them to work "double duty" for some time. It is also a good idea to provide education about change behavior and to do everything possible to recognize and appreciate staff's hard work.

If a health care organization makes the decision to implement the National Learning Lab's recommendations, the decision will no doubt change that organization. However, the effort will be worthwhile since it will move closer to the goal of improving patient safety in facilities throughout the United States and internationally.

Reference

1.   McKee M., Healy J.: The role of the hospital in a changing environment. *Bull World Health Organ* 78(6):803–810, 2000.

2.   James B.: Dealing with the details: Fitting the Business Case in the Current Health Care Environment. Sep. 26–27, 2002. *Building the Business Case for Patient Safety: A Symposium for CEOs,* Arlington, Virginia.

Chapter 10

The Business Case for Facility Design Focused on Patient Safety

"We shape our buildings, and afterwards our buildings shape us." (Winston Churchill, "A Sense of Crowd and Urgency" [speech delivered to the House of Commons, 28 October 1943], in Churchill W.S.: *Never Give In! The Best of Winston Churchill's Speeches*. New York: Hyperion, 2003, p. 358.)

This chapter focuses on the business case for designing a patient-safe facility, beginning with an introduction to the issues involved, including definitions of some key concepts, a discussion of the difficulties associated with building a business case, and recommendations that are essential for a hospital to consider. The business case will consider the impact facility design has on capital, revenues, and operating expenses. In addition, the business case has potential benefits that are more than financial. Safety by design can have a positive effect on staff recruitment and retention, with less staff turnover and increased job satisfaction. Safety by design also impacts the organization's image because safety is seen as a positive, and a better image influences market share.

The business case for patient safety in facility design is complex and should consider two issues:

1. Does an economic investment in resources aimed at lowering error rates result in a return on that investment? This issue focuses on patient safety concerns and their effect on operational profitability.
2. Does the investment in a facility with its technology and equipment focused on patient safety result in a return on investment? This issue focuses on facility development and capital expenditures.

The answers to these questions depend on the constituencies asking the questions. Hospitals, health plans, physician groups, and employees have different answers because their perspectives differ. Furthermore, the business case depends on the interplay of multiple variables, such as capital, operating costs, the payment mechanism, and market and service levels. The business case is made even more complex for provider organizations such as hospitals because of their mission and values.

The Business Case for Patient Safety

In September 2002 The Joint Commission, the American Hospital Association, the Agency for Healthcare Research and Quality, the Veterans Health Administration, and the Centers for Medicare & Medicaid Services sponsored a symposium for hospital CEOs) called "Building the Business Case for Patient Safety." The author was invited to attend the conference and be a member of the final reactor panel entitled "Is the Business Case Built?" The conclusion of the symposium was, in fact, that the business case for patient safety was *not* made, based on the symposium's definition of business case, which was a strict dollars-and-cents return on financial investment.

However, the conference also concluded that there is a moral imperative for an investment in patient safety. It is the mission of hospitals and physician groups to "do no harm" and provide safe, high-quality care. Every hospital and its caregivers would theoretically support the ideal of improving patient safety and investing in it. Some at the conference argued that it is also a market strategy, and improved patient safety and quality could increase market share.

Brent James, M.D., from Intermountain Healthcare (IHC) in Salt Lake City, provided examples of how investing in certain interventions—for example, standardization of presurgical antibiotics at certain times—lowered length of stay, comorbidities, and readmissions of medical patients. Jeff D. Selberg, CEO of Exempla Healthcare in Denver, told a compelling story of his organization's transformation into a quality champion and what impact doing so has had on the market. However, all participants at the conference concluded that those who pay for the patient safety intervention and those who realize the benefits of the patient safety intervention are rarely the same constituency.

This is a significant point to clarify: A basic misalignment of financial incentives exists in health care. Both the fee-for-service payment methodology and the diagnosis-related group payment (DRG) methodology introduce perverse incentives. The care of patients with iatrogenic injuries leads to increased reimbursement under a fee-for-service payment or a DRG payment. The investment in interventions to improve patient safety (for example, to reduce adverse drug events or infections) can actually reduce revenues as a consequence of fewer comorbidities (in the DRG system) or fewer services rendered (in the fee-for-service system). It is possible, though, that the investment in interventions to improve patient safety (for example to reduce infections) can actually lower costs more than any reduction in revenues. Therefore, there could be a business case for patient safety under the DRG system.

If an organization is capitated or is a health plan or a health system that has its own health plan, such as Kaiser Permanente, then the benefits of all patient safety interventions would accrue to the organization. If a health system is not capitated or does not have its own health plan, the improvement in patient safety accrues to the payers and employers, not to the health system making the investment. With capitation, if the insurer pays the hospital on a DRG system, the payer accumulates more money if the hospital is safer, while the hospital receives less money.

Key Concepts

To clarify the situation, a number of key health care financial concepts need to be defined: fee for service, DRG payments, and capitation.

Fee for service—sometimes referred to as discounted fee for service— refers to a payment for a service rendered. For example, a hospital or a physician that provides medications is compensated for the fee charged. Typically a payer, such as Medicare, Medicaid, private insurance companies, self-insured employers, and, less frequently, the patient (as a majority are insured), makes the payment. If less service is provided to the patient because the hospital is "safer," then less medication is dispensed, there are fewer days of care and office visits, and therefore less revenue will be received. This occurs because one must provide services in order to get paid, and the more one provides, the more one gets paid. Unfortunately under this system, it is more profitable to keep patients sick longer than it is to get them well faster.

The *DRG payment methodology* is unique to hospitals. In this system, a fixed amount for a discharge diagnosis is reimbursed. For example, a certain fixed amount is reimbursed if a patient is discharged after having an appendectomy. To receive payment, the hospital needs to admit and then discharge a patient. A set fee is associated with each specific diagnosis. Comorbidities can create a higher payment if the diagnosis has complications, for example, an appendectomy and an infection. The higher the intensity of service, the greater the payment. If a patient safety intervention to lower infection is introduced into a hospital system, the number of comorbidities could decline, in which case a lower DRG payment would occur. But it is also possible that a lower DRG payment is offset by a greater reduction in costs, actually creating more profitability. An example would be investing in high-efficiency particulate air (HEPA) filters throughout the hospital to lower infections. It is common for patients who have been treated in a hospital to unknowingly contract an infection, go home, and then have to be readmitted. Readmissions and extra services provided bring the hospital more revenue. A safer hospital lowers infection rates, so the patient may not get the infection and have to be readmitted; as a result, the hospital loses a second admission and gets paid less.

On the other hand, capitation is enhanced by patient safety initiatives. Capitation means a predetermined amount is paid, usually monthly, for potential services for a patient. Typically, a set of benefits is agreed to for a certain monthly capitation payment. If a patient pays the fee, he or she is covered for potential services whether he or she actually needs them; if the patient doesn't get sick, he or she pays anyway, but if the patient does get sick, treatment is covered. If a patient safety intervention lowers services or admissions or lowers the intensity of services, a capitated organization's financials will improve. The healthier and safer the patients, the less costs because fewer services are being provided and the business can increase its net income.

Most health care payers (such as insurance companies) are capitated, most hospitals are paid for their DRGs, and most physicians are paid by fee-for-service. Therefore, it is clear that if a hospital improves patient safety under a fee-for-service plan or a DRG system, the results could be less revenue from services rendered or fewer DRG payments because of less intensity or fewer admits, resulting in less net income. An example from IHC illustrates this point. IHC invested in an intervention that lowered length of stay (a positive financial impact), but the readmission rate and the comorbidities were also lowered, with an impact greater than the length-of-stay impact. The net impact was that IHC lost money, even though the organization had invested in patient safety. As the payer, Medicare realized the resulting financial return (in saved health costs). Such a situation gives new meaning to the phrase "quality chasm" (usually used to refer to the difference between the care one actually receives and the care it is possible to receive)—in this case, it refers to the chasm between the financial benefits received by payers and by providers.

Barriers to the Business Case

Although the CEOs attending the business case conference agreed with the moral mandate to improve patient safety, they identified several significant barriers to realizing the goal to create a business case:

- First, it is difficult to raise capital for any front-end investment, such as technology that would improve patient safety. Many organizations are living day to day and are not capable of raising capital of any significant amount, and if they could, they would have many conflicting priorities for that capital.

■ A second barrier is aligning the goals of hospital management, especially the CEO, with those of the medical staff. Issues of autonomy and control and lack of physician engagement in the change toward patient safety are paramount. Physicians are not always willing to identify with the organization's goals or to consider specific changes in their own procedures. For example, they may prefer to continue writing orders rather than use computers in an effort to standardize orders. James calls this another type of "quality chasm."

■ A third barrier is lack of information technology infrastructure, which limits the ability to produce data or implement the safety intervention, due to lack of capital, the risk of making a bad investment, and lack of standardization.

■ Another barrier common throughout health care is the culture of blame and shame, rather than a just culture that recognizes human error and appropriate risk behaviors. This is discussed in depth in Chapter 5.

Staffing shortages also cause difficulties. Hospitals are often troubled by staffing shortages, and much time and effort is expended focusing on this urgent need. This leaves less energy to focus on long-term goals such as safety issues.

Hierarchical communication barriers also exist within and outside of hospital organizations. Subgroups within the organization, such as physicians, nurses, pharmacists, and administrators, might not always communicate effectively with each other or even with others within the same subgroup. Outside the organization, communication also can break down between the hospital and payers, hospital medical groups, employers, or the government.

Recommendations for Creating a Business Case

Although the conference participants concluded that a business case could not be supported, they wanted very much to create a business case and looked for recommendations to do so. They believed that the following steps should be taken to create the business case and improve patient safety:

■ **Standardize.** The aviation industry has had success in normalizing pilots' performance expectations through standardization. This standardization has had a positive impact on aviation safety.

■ **Use checklists.** Again, the aviation industry has shown success in using checklists. This recommendation was particularly encouraged during discussions on lowering the incidence of wrong-site surgery.

■ **Use protocols.** Current practice is that a physician provides a set of orders for a patient's treatment based on the diagnosis. In the future, when evidence-based protocols are prepared for each condition, the physicians could use the protocol as their baseline, making exceptions as needed. This is referred to as a negative order, that is, the physician overrides the protocol if necessary and provides a rationale for doing so. However, the physician would not need to write complete individual orders each time; he or she would need to write only any overrides. Protocols should also be applied to transfers or hand offs to lower the potential of miscommunication leading to harm.

■ **Simplify procedures.** In *The Psychology of Everyday Things*, Donald Norman says in effect that when all else fails, standardize and simplify![1] Both standardizing and simplifying reduce costs.

In addition to these general strategies, the following interventions received the greatest support and attention during the breakout sessions of the 2002 symposium:

1. Use medications in unit dose. Many hospitals are already doing this, but many medications are still delivered to hospitals in bulk. Some hospitals still do not use unit dose as much as they could.

2. Mark the surgical site using "time-outs"—right before surgery, everyone stops, double-checks all the pertinent facts about the patient and the surgery required—and/or uses checklists to help. In fact, The Joint Commission requires hospitals to comply with its Universal Protocol for Preventing Wrong Site, Wrong Procedure, Wrong Person Surgery™ as part of the National Patient Safety Goals. Visit http://www.jointcommission.org/NR/rdonlyres/E3C600EB-043B-4E86-B0 4E-CA4A89AD5433/0/universal_protocol.pdf to view the Universal Protocol.

3. Encourage hand washing throughout the hospital to lower infections. Influencing factors to manage include facility design (for example, making sure that sinks are available where needed), providing alcohol-based hand rubs, and planning staffing patterns and schedules so that staff feel they have time to wash their hands as frequently as is required.

4. Use antibiotics, including prophylactic antibiotics, appropriately.

5. Encourage verbal "read backs," in which one person gives an order and another person repeats it back, confirming understanding and compliance.

6. Standardize clinical processes, facilities, equipment, and technology.

7. Empower patients in the core processes.

8. Implement bar coding for medications and other uses.

9. Identify operating room safety officers.

10. Use antibiotic-coated catheters.

11. Implement team training that emulates aviation cockpit crew team training.

12. Use pulse oximetry in the emergency department, obstetrics, and postanesthesia recovery units.

13. Initiate more detailed surgical privileging.

Many of these interventions are process related; some involve facility, equipment, and technology; and all will change the way a hospital operates. It was the opinion of conference participants that, although many if not all of these interventions would save costs, some involve capital investment.

However, since this conference more evidence has emerged on the relationship between safety interventions and costs. For example, some hospitals in Pennsylvania, which were profiled in the TV series *Remaking American Medicine*, have shown that a reduction in infections does lead to improved profitability.[2] In another example, The CMS and Premier, Inc., launched the Hospital Quality Incentive Demonstration Project in 2003, the first national pay-for-performance demonstration of that nature. "Premier's Performance Pays study proves that when evidence-based processes are delivered, quality is higher and costs are lower."[3] So there is an operational business case for safety in certain circumstances.

The Business Case for Facility Development

The business case for facility development has many of the same dynamics as the general business case for patient safety, but with material differences. Currently in health care there are generally two reasons for considering or implementing a facility project, whether new or remodeling:

1. Because existing facilities are obsolete, they often do not provide needed services in the way they formerly did. Many hospital facilities were financed in part by the federal Hill-Burton Act of 1946, and despite any remodeling that has occurred since then, many hospitals have at least the same infra-structure and general design of a 20-year-old hospital with a design that is out of date.
2. The current market needs a different or larger facility. Demand for services shows up in emergency departments exploding with volume, surgical suites that are not large enough, and/or a shortage of beds in growing communities or in organizations with growing market shares. Furthermore, there is a continued significant shift in services from inpatient to outpatient, such as imaging and surgery.

The decision to remodel or build a new hospital is not based on whether the current facilities are patient-safe. Rather, the decisions to build or remodel are market/financial decisions.

The capital necessary to remodel or build new is arrived at based on the need and the ability of the organization to have a return on investment (ROI), or pay back the bonds or mortgage payments on the project. The need is determined by factors such as current waiting lists for services or patients being redirected to other facilities, or by a market-based study. Market-based studies generally assess the population serviced or to be served, calculate a use rate (the amount of demand for that population), and the market share expected for that demand. Then the role and program (the need) is translated into a preliminary capital request. The capital request is integrated into a financial proforma, assessing the proposed revenues, expenses, and the ability to pay off the bonds or mortgages and receive an ROI. The project may be scaled up or down based on this financial analysis. Before the project starts, the organization has decided that the project is financially feasible (has an ROI) and that it can pay back the bonds.

Another issue related to the business case for facility development focused on safety is the impact on capital—does designing a safe hospital require more capital? It is true that certain design features that could affect latent conditions and active failures require more capital than a traditional hospital design. For example, HEPA filters for the entire hospital cost more than traditional filter systems. However, many proposed design features aimed at patient safety are not any more expensive than a traditional design. An example would be deciding where to put the bathroom in a patient room; two possibilities would likely cost the same, but one location would be safer for the patient. Some standardized design features focused on patient safety will reduce costs.

In all cases, an organization can live within the capital available and design a hospital facility project focused on patient safety. In other words, if an organization decides on a project and settles on a capital amount, then it has already decided it can afford that project. After that, the organization needs to prioritize the design features to enhance safety within the capital available. The key is to prioritize design features within whatever capital amount is available to the organization. With that focus, a safe hospital can be built within the capital budget.

The impact on revenues and operating expenses is more complex. A safer hospital will have less harm because, for example, fewer medication errors will eliminate waste and rework (that is, fixing or re-doing a process that could have led to patient harm). Therefore, the safer hospital will use fewer resources per patient stay. If a hospital is being reimbursed on a fee-for-service system, it is being reimbursed for harm and the resulting rework and waste. Because a safer hospital will use fewer resources, it will also receive less reimbursement, which typically leads to reduced net income. Under the DRG system, it is also possible this could lead to enhanced net income: The revenues would remain the same or less, but the costs would decline to a greater degree.

At the same time, it is important to note that the reduction in harm, rework, and waste will also reduce the length of stay. Instead of a patient staying an extra day or half day because of a medication error, in a safer environment with less error, the patient goes home sooner. This would allow addition-al patients to be admitted, raising the revenues, expenses, and net income. The net income impact should be greater in a safer hospital than in a traditional hospital because the service levels are greater, with more admissions; therefore, the revenue is greater per fixed expenses. But one important condition needs to be met for this to happen: Patients must be available to be admitted. If market share is considered during the financial feasibility stage, this should be possible (although not always). If the increased patient demand is not available for the capacity, the ROI of the capital will not occur.

For most hospitals, the strong majority of the revenue is DRG based. If, as a result of creating a safer environment, less error and harm occur, the rework savings, length-of-stay gains, and lower resources all lower expenses while the revenue stays constant, except for one circumstance—the change in the discharge DRG as the result of no comorbidity. When this happens, it is possible that the loss in DRG payments may be greater than the cost savings. Again, a safer hospital will have less readmission and shorter lengths of stay, so additional volume (admissions) needs to occur to fill the capacity, or the business case doesn't exist. To be financially viable, the volume of available patients is crucial. If the volume (admissions) is available, the overall increase in net income resulting from these factors will be greater than the loss resulting from lower DRG payments because of comorbidity changes.

A hospital focused on safety should also be more efficient, regardless of the payment source. Stan-dardization, minimizing fatigue, and a focus on human factors should create an environment in which, coupled with simplified revised processes to focus on safety, work can be done more efficiently. Productivity should be improved, lowering costs. The hours of care of employees per service rendered should improve (for example, if one assumes it usually takes 10 hours for a certain service, then in more efficient conditions, the time could be reduced to just 8 hours). The result would be lowered costs while maintaining revenue, all of which increases net income.

St. Joseph's Hospital of West Bend, Wisconsin, has met the criteria for creating a business case for designing around patient safety. The capital budget that was originally developed when the organiza-tion contemplated a traditional facility development was $55 million. When the focus shifted to patient safety in design, the capital costs were under $55 million. In fact, because the project was under budget, it was possible to add additional Role and Program (discussed in Chapter 4). The concerns about whether a focus on safety in design would expend greater capital than a traditional hospital design did not materialize, mainly through a thoughtful process sparked by the matrix development design process (discussed in Chapter 3).

The St. Joseph's market is one of the fastest growing in Wisconsin. Serving primarily Washington County, it has been ranked as one of the top five growing counties in the state. If St. Joseph's can capture some of that growth or grow the market share, as predicted, then the volume of patient admissions needed to fill the capacity created by a safer hospital will exist. Improved service levels around many specialties, a new location, and robust physician recruitment should also improve the likelihood of increased market share.

The St. Joseph's payment mechanism is mainly DRG, but it still has significant fee-for-service contracts. Some concerns have been expressed regarding the fee-for-service contracts. For example, if a hospital is being paid on a fee-for-service basis, it is being paid for the amount of harm that occurs—that is, it receives more money if patients stay longer. It would follow that if a hospital improves safety, it would receive less money. The financial outcomes of a safe hospital are stronger under a DRG payment methodology but also exist under the fee-for-service system. Under the DRG system, a hospital is paid a fixed amount for a diagnosis. Therefore, if the hospital has the same volume of patients, the business case would work only if the hospital increases volume—that is, if it can attract more patients. The length of stay and cost per discharge are two indicators that St. Joseph's hopes to improve as a result of designing around patient safety. Shorter lengths of stays, less waste and rework, and improved efficiency, coupled with the availability of increased volumes and capital consistent with the forecast would create the business case for St. Joseph's.

It is worth reinforcing an additional benefit contemplated as a result of focusing on safety in design—enhanced recruitment and retention of staff. Because staff were involved during the design stages, the result is a hospital that works better for staff. Less fatigue, improved technology, standardization, and less "catch and fetch" (wasting time trying to find things or contacting the necessary personnel) lead to lower error rates and improved patient outcomes. This is an environment that ideally will entice caregivers to work there and encourage existing staff to stay. Better staff retention saves costs associated with recruitment, orientation, training, and "learning curve" inefficiencies associated with continued staff turnover. Safety by design has another potential benefit: improved image. It is a benefit to have safety as an organization's primary concern, which often results in an improved market share for that organization.

Although the business case for patient safety does not yet exist, the business case for facilities designed for safety does exist, given certain conditions. These conditions are managing within the capital budget consistent with a traditional design, and increased volume to fill capacity created by a safer facility.

To significantly improve the safety of patients and staff in a hospital is a transforming process. Facilities with their equipment and technology, process, and safety culture all need to significantly change. This book is meant to be a guide through this critical transformation, so that safety and quality of patient care in health care are enhanced.

References

1. Norman D.A.: *The Psychology of Everyday Things.* New York: Basic Books, 1988.

2. *Remaking American Medicine™. . . Healthcare for the 21st Century.* A PBS four-part series produced by Crossroads Media, broadcast Oct. 2006. http://www.ramcampaign.org/pages/aboutRAM.htm (accessed May 30, 2007).

3. Premier, Inc.: *Pay for Performance: Premier's Pay-for-Performance Study.* http://www.premierinc.com/quality-safety/tools-services/p4p/index.jsp (accessed May 30, 2007).

Bibliography

Adverse Health Events in Minnesota: Third Annual Report. St. Paul, Minnesota Department of Health, Jan. 2007.

American Institute of Architects: *Guidelines for Design and Construction of Hospital and Health Care Facilities.* Washington, DC: AIA Press, 2001.

American Medical Association (AMA): *Report of the Board of Trustees on Medication Errors in Hospitals.* Chicago: AMA, Jun. 1994.

Andrews L.N., et al.: An alternative strategy for studying adverse events in medical care. *Lancet* 349:309–313, Feb. 1, 1997.

Ashton C.M.: Geographic variation in utilization rates in Veterans Affairs hospitals and clinics. *N Engl J Med* 280:32–39, Jan. 7, 1999.

Bartlett F.C.: *Remembering: A Study in Experimental and Social Psychology.* Cambridge: Cambridge University Press, 1921.

Bates D.W., et al.: Incidence of adverse drug events and potential adverse drug events. *JAMA* 275:29–34, Jul. 1995.

Bates D.W., et al.: Relationship between medication errors and adverse drug events. *J Gen Intern Med* 10:199–205, Apr. 1995.

Berens R.J.: Noise in the pediatric intensive care unit. *J Intensive Care Med* 14:118–129, Jun. 1999.

Berwick D.M.: *Keynote Address Presented at the 11th National Forum on Quality Improvement in Healthcare.* VHS. New Orleans: Institute for Healthcare Improvement, Dec. 7, 1999.

Blendon R.J., et al.: Views of practicing physicians and the public on medical errors. *N Engl J Med* 347:1933–1940, Dec. 12, 2002.

Brennan T.A., et al.: The incidence of adverse events and negligence in hospitalized patients: Results of the Harvard Medical Practice Study, I. *N Engl J Med* 324:370–376, Feb. 7, 1991.

Bridge Medical, Inc.: *Beyond Blame Documentary.* VHS. Huntingdon Valley, PA: Institute of Safe Medication Practices, 1998.

Bridges W.: *Managing Transitions.* Cambridge, MA: Da Capo Press, Perseus Books Group, 2003.

Bromley D.B.: Academic contributions to psychological counseling: A philosophy of science for the study of individual cases. *Counseling Psychology Quarterly* 3:299–307, 1990.

Bullough J., Rea M.S.: Lighting for neonatal intensive care units: Some critical information of design. *Lighting Research and Technology* 28(4):189–198, 1996.

Bunker J.P., Wennberg J.E.: Operational rates, mortality statistics and the quality of life. *N Engl J Med* 289:1249–1250, Dec. 6, 1973.

Busch A., Fawcett M.D., Jacobs D.G.: Clinical correlates of inpatient suicides. *J Clin Psychiatry* 64:14–19, Jan. 2003.

Cameron K.S., Quinn R.E.: *Diagnosing and Changing Organizational Culture: Based on the Competing Values Framework,* rev. ed. San Francisco: Jossey-Bass, 2006.

Centers for Disease Control and Prevention (National Center for Health Statistics): Births and deaths: Preliminary data for 1998. *National Vital Statistics Reports* 47:1–46, Oct. 9, 1999.

Churchill W.: A sense of crowd and urgency. Speech delivered to the House of Commons, London, Oct. 28, 1943. In Churchill, W.: *Never Give In! The Best of Winston Churchill's Speeches.* New York: Hyperion, 2003.

de Jong R.G., et al.: *Proceedings of the 8th International Congress on Noise as a Public Health Problem.* Jun. 29–Jul. 3, 2003. Foundation ICBEN 2003 Congress, Rotterdam, Netherlands.

Denham C.R.: From harmony to healing: Join the quality choir. *Journal of Patient Safety* 2:225–232, Dec. 2006.

DeRosier J., et al.: Using health care failure mode and effects analysis: The VA National Center for patient safety's prospective risk analysis system. *Jt Comm J Qual Patient Saf* 28:248–267, May 2002.

Dickerman K., Nevo I., Barach P.: Incorporating patient-safe design into the guidelines. *Journal of the American Institute of Architecture,* Oct. 19, 2005.

Drucker P.F.: What executives should remember. *Harv Bus Rev* 84:144–152, Feb. 2006.

Dubois R.W., Brook, R.H.: Preventable deaths: Who, how often and why? *Ann Intern Med* 109:582–589, Oct. 1, 1988.

Eisenhardt K.M.: Building theories from case study research. *Academy of Management Review* 14:532–550, Oct. 1989.

Epstein A.: Pay for performance at the tipping point. *N Eng J Med* 356:515–517, Jan. 26, 2007.

Fendrick A.M., Ridker P., Bloom D.: Improved health benefits of increased use of thrombolytic therapy. *Arch Intern Med* 154:1605–1609, Jul. 25, 1994.

Figueiro M.G., Eggleston G., Rea M.S.: Effects of light exposure on behavior of Alzheimer's patients—A pilot study. Light and Human Health: EPRI/LRO 5th International Lighting Research Symposium. Palo Alto, CA: The Lighting Research Office of the Electric Power Research Institute, pp. 151–156, 2002.

Figueiro M.G., Rea M.S.: New research in the light and health field is expanding the possibilities for LED lighting in healthcare environments. In *CIE Midterm Meeting Conference Proceedings.* Leon: Spain, 2005.

Fonarow G.C., et al.: Association between performance measures and clinical outcomes for patients hospitalized with heart failure. *JAMA* 297:61–70, Jan. 3, 2007.

Fullan M.: *Leading in a Culture of Change.* San Francisco: Jossey-Bass, 2001.

General Electric: *GE Lighting Healthcare.* http://www.gelighting.com/na/business_lighting/lighting_applications/healthcare/index.htm (accessed Jul. 2, 2007).

General Motors Corporation, *Potential Failure Mode and Effects Analysis (FMEA): Reference Manual.* 3rd ed., Detroit, 2001.

Guidelines for Intensive Care Unit Design. Guidelines/Practice Parameters Committee of the American College of Critical Care Medicine, Society of Critical Care Medicine. *Crit Care Med* 23:582–588, Mar. 1995.

Herzlinger R.E.: Why innovation in health care is so hard. *Harv Bus Rev* 84:58–66, May 2006.

Institute of Medicine: *Patient Safety: Achieving a New Standard for Care.* Washington, DC: National Academy Press, 2004.

Institute of Medicine: *Crossing the Quality Chasm: A New Health System for the 21st Century.* Washington, DC: National Academy Press, 2001.

Institute of Medicine: *To Err Is Human: Building A Safer Health System.* Washington, DC: National Academy Press, 1999.

Institute of Medicine National Roundtable on Health Care Quality: The urgent need to improve health care quality. *JAMA* 280:1000–1005, Sep. 16, 1998.

Jha, A.K., Duncan B., and Bates D.: Fatigue, sleepiness, and medical errors. In Shojania K., et al. (eds.): *Making Health Care Safer: Critical Analysis of Patient Safety Practices.* Agency for Healthcare Research and Quality, 2002. http://www.ahrq.gov/clinic/ptsafety/chap45.htm (accessed May 29, 2007).

Joint Commission: *Sentinel Event Statistics: As of December 31, 2006.* http://www.jointcommission.org/NR/rdonlyres/74540565-4D0F-4992-863E-8F9E949E6B56/0/se_stats_0331.pdf (accessed May 29, 2007).

Joint Commission: Infection control related sentinel events. *Sentinel Event Alert 28, Jan. 22, 2003.* http://www.jointcommission.org/SentinelEvents/SentinelEventAlert/sea_28.htm (accessed May 29, 2007).

Joint Commission: Fatal falls: Lesson for the future. *Sentinel Event Alert* 14, Jul. 12,2000. http://www.jointcommission.org/SentinelEvents/SentinelEventAlert/sea_14.htm (accessed May 29, 2007).

Joint Commission: Inpatient suicides: Recommendations for prevention. *Sentinel Event Alert* 7, Nov. 6, 1998. http://www.jointcommission.org/SentinelEvents/SentinelEventAlert/sea_7.htm (accessed May 29, 2007).

Johnson J.A., Bootman J.L.: Drug-related morbidity and mortality: A cost-of-illness model. *Arch Intern Med* 155 18:1949–1956, Oct. 9, 1995.

Joseph A.: The Impact of Light on Outcomes in Healthcare Settings. The Center for Health Design. Aug. 2006. http://www.healthdesign.org/research/reports/documents/CHD_Issue_Paper2.pdf (accessed May 29, 2007).

Kleeman W.B. Jr.: *The Challenge of Interior Design.* New York: Van Nostrand Reinhold, 1983.

Knox R.A.: Anguish: Inquiry at Dana-Farber. *Boston Globe* Mar. 23, 1995.

Leape L.: Error in medicine. *JAMA* 272:1851–1857, Aug. 9, 1994.

Leape L., et al.: Preventing Medical Injury. *Quality Review Bulletin* 19:144–149, May 1993.

Leape L., et al.: The nature of adverse events in hospitalized patients: Results of the Harvard Medical Practice Study, II. *N Engl J Med* 324:377–384, Feb. 7, 1991.

Lefevre F., et al.: Iatrogenic complications in high-risk, elderly patients. *Arch Intern Med* 152: 2074–2080, Oct. 1992.

Lesar T.S., Briceland L., Stein D.: Factors related to errors in medication prescribing. *JAMA* 277:312–317, Jan. 22, 1997.

Lesar T.S., et al.: Medication prescribing errors in a teaching hospital. *Arch Intern Med* 157:1569–1576, Jul. 28, 1997.

Liker J.K. : *The Toyota Way: 14 Management Principles from the World's Greatest Manufacturer.* New York: McGraw-Hill, 2004.

Lindenauer P.K., et al.: Public reporting and pay for performance in hospital quality improvement. *N Engl J Med* 356:486–496, Feb. 1, 2007.

Longo D.R., et al.: The long road to patient safety. *JAMA* 294:2858–2865, Dec. 14, 2006.

Manasse H.R. Jr.: Medication use in an imperfect world: Drug misadventuring as an issue of public policy, part 1. *Am J Hosp Pharm* 46: 929–944, May 1989.

Marck P.B., et al.: Building safer systems by ecological design: Using restoration science to develop a medication safety intervention. *Qual Saf Health Care* 15:1592–1597, Apr. 2006.

Marshall M. Jr.: The physician's role in health facility planning. *Pa Medicine* 70:81–82, Jun. 1967.

Mau B.: *Massive Change.* London: Phaidon Press, 2004.

McKee M., Healy J.: The role of the hospital in a changing environment. *Bull World Health Organ* 78:803–810, 2000.

Millenson M.: *Demanding Medical Excellence.* Chicago: University of Chicago Press, 1997.

Mills D.H.: Medical insurance feasibility study—A technical summary. *West J Med* 128:360–365, Apr. 1978.

Moray N.: Error reduction as a systems problem. In Bogner M.S. (ed.): *Human Error in Medicine.* Boca Raton, FL: CRC Press, 1994, pp. 67–91.

Morrison W., et al.: Noise, stress and annoyance in a pediatric intensive care unit. *Crit Care Med* 30:113–119, Jan. 2003.

Murthy V.S.S.N., et al.: Detrimental effects of noise on anaesthetists. *Can J Anaesth* 42:608–611, Jul. 1995.

National Patient Safety Foundation, American Medical Association: *Agenda for Research and Development in Patient Safety.* Updated May 24, 1999. http://npsf.org/pdf/r/researchagenda.pdf (accessed May 29, 2007).

Norman D. A.: *The Psychology of Everyday Things.* New York: Basic Books, 1988.

Partnerships for Patient Safety: *First Do No Harm, Part 1: A Case Study of Systems Failures.* VHS. Chicago: Partnerships for Patient Safety, 2003.

Perrow C.: *Normal Accidents: Living with High-Risk Technologies.* New York: Basic Books, 1984.

Piergeorge A.R., Cesarano F.L., Casanova D.M.: Designing the critical care unit: A multi-disciplinary approach. *Crit Care Med* 11:541–545, Jul. 1983.

Piper B.F., et al.: The revised Piper Fatigue Scale: Psychometric evaluation in women with breast cancer. *Oncol Nurs Forum* 25:677–684, May 1998.

Pronovost P.J., Miller M.R., Wachter R.M.: Tracking progress in patient safety. *JAMA* 296:696–699, Aug. 9, 2006.

Pyecha J.: *A Case Study of the Application of Noncategorical Special Education in Two States.* Chapel Hill, NC: Research Triangle Institute, 1988.

Rashid M.: A decade of adult intensive care unit design: A study of the physical design features of the best-practice examples. *Crit Care Nurs Q* 29:282–311, Oct. 2006.

Rasmussen J.: Skills, rules, knowledge: Signals, signs, and symbols, and other distinctions in human performance models. *IEEE Transactions on Systems, Man, and Cybernetics* 13:257–266, May–Jun., 1983.

Rasmussen J., Jensen A.: Mental procedures in real-life tasks: A case study of electronic troubleshooting. *Ergonomics* 17:293–307, May 1974.

Rasmussen J., Pedersen O.: Human factors in probabilistic risk analysis and risk management. In *Operational Safety of Nuclear Power Plants 1.* Vienna: International Atomic Energy Agency, 1984.

Reiling J.G., et al.: Enhancing the traditional hospital design process: A focus on patient safety. *Jt Comm J Qual Patient Saf* 30:115–124, May 2004.

Reason J.: *Managing the Risks of Organizational Accidents.* Aldershot, UK: Ashgate Publishing, 1997.

Reason J.: *Human Error.* Cambridge MA: Cambridge University Press, 1990.

Reason J., Hobbs A.: *Managing Maintenance Error: A Practical Guide.* Aldershot, UK: Ashgate Publishing, 2003.

Risk Management Guidelines: Companion to AS/NZS 4360. Standards Australia / Standards New Zealand. Sydney, Australia, Australian Standard, 2004.

Rose J.S., et al.: A leadership framework for culture change in health care. *Jt Comm J Qual Patient Saf* 32:433–442, Aug. 2006.

Rosenthal M.M., Sutcliffe K.M. (eds): *Medical Error: What Do We Know? What Do We Do?* San Francisco: Jossey-Bass, 2002.

Roth G.K., Kleiner A.: *Car Launch: The Human Side of Managing Change.* New York: Oxford University Press, 2000.

Rouse W. B.: Models of human problem solving: Detection, diagnosis and compensation for system failures. In Johannsen G.: *Proceedings of IFAC Conference On Analysis, Design and Evaluation of Man-Machine Systems.* Amsterdam: Pergamon, 1983.

Sandy L.G.: Homeostasis without reserve—The risk of health system collapse. *N Engl J Med* 347:1971–1975, Apr. 3, 2003.

Schein E.H.: *Career Anchors: Self Assessment,* 3rd ed. San Francisco: Pfeiffer, 2006.

Schein E. H. *Organizational Culture and Leadership,* 3rd ed. San Francisco: Jossey-Bass, 2004.

Schimmel E. M.: The hazards of hospitalization. *Ann Intern Med* 60:100–110, Jan. 1964.

Senge P.S., et al.: *Presence: Human Purpose and the Field of the Future,* Cambridge, MA: The Society for Organizational Learning, Inc., 2004.

Shojania K.G., et al.: *Making Health Care Safer: Critical Analysis of Patient Safety Practices.* Agency for Healthcare Research and Quality. 2002. http://www.ahrq.gov/clinic/ptsafety/chap45.htm (accessed May 29, 2007)

Soumerai S.B., et al.: Adverse outcome of underuse of beta-blockers in elderly survivors of acute myocardial infarction. *JAMA* 277:115–121, Jan. 8, 1997.

Stamatis D.H.: *Failure Mode and Effects Analysis.* Milwaukee: American Society of Quality Press, 1995.

Steel K., et al.: Iatrogenic illness on a general medical service at a university hospital. *N Engl J Med* 304:638–642, Mar. 1981.

Swaim T.J.: Staff involvement in critical care unit construction. *Crit Care Med* 14:63–70, May 1991.

Tellis W.: Introduction to case study. *The Qualitative Report* 3:1–11, Jul. 1997.

Thomas E., et al.: Costs of medical injuries in Utah and Colorado. *Inquiry* 36:255–264, Fall 1999.

Turner K.: *Integrated Risk and Safety Management.* Sydney, Australia: The Aerosafe Group, 2006.

Ulrich R., Zimring C.: The role of the physical environment in the hospital of the 21st Century: A once-in-a-lifetime opportunity. Report to The Center for Health Design, for the Designing for the 21st Century Hospital Project, Sep. 2004.

Voelker R.: "Pebbles" cast ripples in health care design. *JAMA* 286:1701–1702, Oct. 10, 2001.

Wachter R.M., Shojania K.G.: *Internal Bleeding: The Truth Behind America's Terrifying Epidemic of Medical Mistakes,* 2nd ed. New York: Rugged Land, LLC, 2004.

Walch J.M., et al.: The effect of sunlight on post-operative analgesic medication usage: A prospective study of spinal surgery patients. *Psychosomatic Medicine* 67:156–163, Jan.–Feb. 2005.

Weinger M.B.: Incorporating human factors into the design of medical devices. *JAMA* 280:1484, Nov. 4, 1984.

Wennberg J.E., et al.: Hospital use and mortality among Medicare beneficiaries in Boston and New Haven. *N Engl J Med* 321:1168–1173, Oct. 26, 1989.

Winters B.D., Pham J., Pronovost P.J.: Rapid response teams—Walk, don't run. *JAMA* 296:1645–1647, Oct. 4, 2006.

Yin R.K.: *Case Study Research: Design and Methods,* 2nd ed. Beverly Hills, CA: Sage Publishing, 1994.

Index

A

Accountability, 97

Active failures
   as cause of errors, 5–6, 12–13, 70
   definition, 5–6, 52
   design impact on patient safety checklist, 65
   examples of, 5, 18, 52
   patient room design and, 107–108
   reasons for, 6
   significance and impact of, 52–56, 111
   Swiss cheese model of safety, 8

Adaptability, 48, 63, 105

ADEs (adverse drug events), 51

Adjacencies (block diagrams)
   conceptual design phase, 77, 78, 79, 80
   dFMEA, 38, 40–42
   function of, 34

Administration of medication, rights of, 66

Adverse drug events (ADEs), 51

Adverse events. *See also* Medical errors
   causes of, 6, 8, 13
   definition, 6
   prevalence of, 89
   report on preventable events, 86, 89

Affordance, 30

Agency for Healthcare Research and Quality (AHRQ)
   "Building the Business Case for Patient Safety" conference, 115
   Hospital Survey on Patient Safety Culture, 89
   Patient Safety Climate Survey, 46

AHA (American Hospital Association), 115

AHRQ. *See* Agency for Healthcare Research and Quality (AHRQ)

AIA (American Institute of Architects), 70, 104

Air movement in patient rooms, 53, 76

Alcoves, 52, 102, 103

American Hospital Association (AHA), 115

American Institute of Architects (AIA)
   document B141, 70
   "Guidelines for Design and Construction of Health Care Facilities" (Facilities Guidelines Institute), 104

Architect's role in design process
   "Safe by Design" approach, 69–70, 72–84
   traditional approach, 69, 70–72

Automation, 50–51, 62, 106. *See also* Technology

Aviation industry
   accident rate, 13
   checklists, 46
   Line Operation Safety Audits, 91
   non-jeopardy reporting, 90–91
   risk and safety management, 91–92
   spaceflight aviation, 14–16\

B

Bar code technology, 23, 54

Batching process, 27–28

Beliefs, shared, 58–59, 98, 110–111

Bids for construction, 72, 83

Blame-free environment, 59, 90–91

Block diagrams. See Adjacencies (block diagrams)

Blood transfusion process, 55, 108

Bronson Methodist Hospital, 104

Budgets for construction
   business case for facilities designed for safety and, 120–122
   calculating construction costs, 33
   calculating constructions costs, 83
   design decisions and, 73
   matrix development process, 35, 36

D

Daylight, benefits of, 49

Design, measure, analyze, improve, and control (DMAIC), 25

Design development phase, 34, 42, 43–44, 72, 82–83

Design failure mode and effects analysis (dFMEA), 38, 40–44

Design of facilities. See Facility design

DFMEA (design failure mode and effects analysis), 38, 40–44

Diagnosis-related group payment (DRG) method, 116, 117, 121, 122

DMAIC (design, measure, analyze, improve, and control), 25

E

Education and training of staff, 61, 87, 91–92, 99

Electrical-systems design, 76, 106

Emergency department operational processes plan, 74

Equipment planning, 45, 77, 106

Error, definition of, 5

"Error in Medicine" (Leape), 4

Error proofing, 30–31

Executive walk-arounds, 61

F

Facilities Guidelines Institute, 104

Facility design. *See also* Facility design process
active failures and (see Active failures)
barriers to effective design, 111–113
business case for facilities designed for safety, 120–122
culture of safety and, 14, 18, 19, 67

design principles, 21–22
error prevention through, 16, 17–19
human error and, 2–3, 13
latent conditions and (see Latent conditions)
measurement of principles, 46
outcomes of care and, vii, 3
patient safety and, vii, 34
requirements for, 109–111
safety-driven design principles, 34–47
spaceflight aviation comparison, 14–16
strategies to support safety design process, 22–24
    checklist, 61, 62–66
studies on, vii, 3

Facility design process
architect's role in
    "Safe by Design" approach, 69–70, 72–84
    traditional approach, 69, 70–72
leadership's role in, 24, 32, 109–110
physicians' role in, 32, 85, 86, 92, 95–96, 98–99
review of core processes, 23–24
staff involvement in, 24, 32, 110, 112–113
stakeholders in, 109, 110, 111
steps in, vii–viii, 17, 33–34
time allotment for, 82

Failure mode and effects analysis (FMEA), 37–44, 64

Fall prevention, 55, 108

Families of patients
involvement in care decisions, 66
involvement in design process, 44–45, 111

Fatigue
fatigue scale survey, 46
minimizing, 51, 64, 106
of physicians, 87–88, 99

Fee-for-service payment method, 116, 117, 122

Financial impact of safety by design, 112, 120–122

Financial incentives in health care, 116

Five rights of medication administration, 66

Five Ss, 26

Flexibility, 48, 63, 105

Flooring, 105

T

U

V

W